Cornet Drake

Presented by

A. Adair Esq.

A MANUAL

FOR

VOLUNTEER CORPS

OF

CAVALRY.

LONDON:

PRINTED FOR THE WAR-OFFICE,

BY T. EGERTON, AT THE MILITARY LIBRARY, NEAR
WHITEHALL.

1803.

Horfe-Guards,
22d *November,* 1803.

THE following Inftructions are recommended by His Royal Highnefs the COMMANDER IN CHIEF, for the ufe of the feveral Corps of Yeomanry and Volunteer Cavalry, throughout the United Kingdom.

By His Royal Highnefs's Command,

HARRY CALVERT,
Adjutant-General.

CONTENTS.

CONTENTS.

CONTENTS.

T A B L E

EXPLAINING THE

SEVERAL FIGURES, MARKS, &c.

The STANDARD—denotes the Front.

POINTED ARROW—the Direction of the Movement.

DOTTED LINES—the March of different Bodies.

BLUNTED ARROW—the Markers neceſſary to determine the Wheel, &c. &c.

MOUNTED FIGURES—the new Direction and Poſition in Line.

SQUARE DOTS—Squadron Officers.

ROUND DOTS—Diviſion Leaders.

ABSTRACT

FROM

HIS MAJESTY's REGULATIONS

FOR THE

FORMATIONS AND MOVEMENTS

OF THE

C A V A L R Y.

S. 1. *Formation of Squadron and Regiment.*

THE SQUADRONS of cavalry are compofed each of two troops.

REGIMENTS are compofed of two, three, or more fquadrons.

A LINE is compofed of two or more regiments.

A fquadron formed in line with the files at fix inches from boot-top to boot-top, occupies in front nearly as many yards as it has files, or about thirty-four inches for each horfe.

In regiment or line, the fquadrons are formed with an interval betwixt each, equal to one third of their actual front.

All the various movements of the fquadron, or larger body, are compounded of *Paffaging* and *Reining back*—*Dreffing*—*Marching in front*—*Wheeling*—*Filing*—*Inclining*. General movements of the fqua-dron.

S. 2. *Paſſaging and Reining back.*

Paſſaging. Paſſaging and reining back, are leſſons of the manage, and neceſſary in opening or cloſing of ranks, files, or intervals of ſquadrons.

When ground is to be taken to the flank by paſſaging, the whole body moves at the word To the—— pass! and halts at the word Halt! and therefore ſucceſſive movement of files is not to be permitted, nor will it be attempted if the command is given in a ſtrong and decided tone.

Reining back. In reining back of bodies or ranks, the whole look to the hand to which they ought to form or dreſs; the movement is never to be hurried; to be made in order and the horſes to be kept ſtraight.

S. 3. *Dreſſing.*

Dreſſing. Dreſſing is occaſional to right, center, or left, as ordered.

The ſqua- dron and all bodies till otherwiſe ordered,

Dreſs	To the hand to which they form.
March	To the hand to which they were dreſſed when halted.
Halt	To the hand to which they were dreſſed when marching.

When the entire ſquadron moves in line, or wheels, *dreſſing* is to the ſtandard in the center.

When a column of entire ſquadrons marches in an alignement, in order to wheel up and form line, *dreſſing* and covering, as in other ſimilar columns, is to the pivot flank.

In *dreſſing* the horſes muſt ſtand ſtraight to the front, and the men's bodies muſt be ſquare, each juſt caſting his eye along his next man's face but without turning his head. The men muſt be uniformly placed on horſe-back, for on this ſquareneſs of man and horſe both dreſſing and movement moſt eſſentially depend.

All *dreſſing* is to be made with as much alacrity of
officers

officers and foldiers as poffible, and the dreffer of each body as he accomplifhes the operation will give a caution, *Front!* that heads may then be replaced and remain fquare to the front. If the body to be dreffed is extenfive, the dreffer muft juftly place one divifion before he proceeds on that which is beyond it.

Every *dreffer* of a body in a given line, muft in his own perfon be placed on that line, while he is directing fuch operation.

S. 4. *Marching in Front.*

The fquadron being fuppofed halted and dreffed, the *leader* muft take care that he is exactly placed before the ftandard, and fquare with refpect to the front of the fquadron, or the general line. In this pofition from habit, and with a glance of the eye, he determines the perpendicular direction which he is to follow, and cannot fail to remark two or more fmall objects on the ground, which are in the line of his direction. Marching in line.
Line of march taken.

The leader gives the word, THE SQUADRON WILL ADVANCE! as a caution—at the word MARCH! each man cafts his eyes to the ftandard, puts his horfe in motion, and dreffes with the greateft exactnefs to the ftandard, and non-commiffioned officer that covers it. Advance of the fquadron.

The attention of the *ftandard-bearer* is to keep a horfe's length from the leader, to follow him exactly and fcrupuloufly, and flacken or quicken his pace according to the words of command or direction he receives. This muft be done gradually, and without hurrying or fpringing forward, which will always occafion a fhake in the fquadron. Attention of ftandard.

The attention of the reft of the fquadron is invariably fixed on the center; that of the front rank on the ftandard; and that of the rear rank on the non-commiffioned officer covering it, who gives the diftance of ranks as ordered. Attention of the ranks.

As

As the great bufinefs of every leader of a fquadron
is to carry it forward in its exact perpendicular direction, it requires his whole attention. The ftandard,
officers, and ferrefiles, muft take care that the fquadron
is dreffed, and up to its leader, who muft not be looking back to give fuch directions, otherwife he will undoubtedly fwerve, and not conduct it with that fteadinefs which is fo effential, efpecially in relative movements, and which depend entirely upon himfelf.

If a fmall alteration is to be made in the *direction* of
the fquadron, the leader gradually circles into fuch
new direction, with which the fquadron complies by
advancing one flank and retaining the other, till the
change is effected, and a ftraight line refumed.

When the word HALT! is given, the whole halt by
the center. The word DRESS! inftantaneoufly follows,
and the file on each fide of the ftandard diligently conforming to the general direction, gives the line to the
reft of the fquadron, who immediately, if neceffary,
correct the diftance of files.

If one movement is immediately to fucceed another,
a critical dreffing need not be required, and the fquadron may remain looking to the center, till the order
for marching is again given.

S. 5. Wheeling.

WHEELING is one of the moft effential and important operations of the fquadron, neceffary in many
changes of pofition and in the formations of column
and of the line.

When the entire fquadron is to wheel, a caution is
given to that purport, and to which hand. At the
word MARCH! the front rank of the fquadron remains
dreffed to the center, the leader fixes his eye, and
makes his circle on the ftanding flank man; the ftandard follows him exactly, and the fquadron wheels
with the fame uniform front, at fuch a pace as is requifite to keep every where dreffed with the ftandard.
                                                      The

The rear rank and the ferrefiles look to the wheeling flank, and incline at the fame time that they wheel, fo as always to cover their front leaders.

The *ftandard* muft take care never to oblige the wheeling man to exceed a moderate gallop, otherwife the rear rank, which has ftill more ground to go over, cannot keep up, the fquadron will wheel loofe and in diforder, and be longer in dreffing, than if it had come about at a flower pace, but clofe and connected. Attention of ftand- ard.

· · The *flanks* muft always conform to the center, in cafe the leader does not take his ground as exactly as he ought. At any rate the ftandard is the guide for the pace, and to preferve the diftance of files from. Attention of the flanks.

The leader muft take care to time his words, HALT! DRESS! the inftant before the wheel is completed, other-wife an overwheel or reining back will be the confe-quence. The whole halt and drefs by the center. Halt of the fquadron.

In all divifion wheelings, the whole look to the wheeling hand. In all wheelings, the rear rank muft rein back at the ftanding flank, and incline towards the wheeling hand in order to cover. Rear rank.

At the words, HALT! DRESS! given when the wheel is completed, the whole turn eyes, and drefs to the ftanding flank, and remain fo until a new direction is given. Halt of di-vifions.

The diftances of divifions of the fquadron when in column, are taken and preferved from front rank to front rank. Diftances in column after wheeling.

In divifion wheelings, the whole keep clofed lightly towards the hand they wheel to, and muft avoid prefs-ing the pivot man off his ground. The outward flank man looks to his rank, he of courfe, regulates the pace at which the wheel is made, he muft not prefs in on his rank, nor turn his horfe's head towards the ftanding flank, all the horfes heads muft be kept rather outwards, (for to attempt to bend them inwards would certainly occafion a crowding on the ftanding flank), and the croupes lightly clofed inwards with the leg. The pivot man of the wheel turns his horfe on his forefeet, keeps his ground, and comes gradually round with his rank. Attention in wheels of divi-fions.

B 3   Although

On a halt-
ed pivot.

Although in the completion of the wheel in column on a halted pivot, the paufe made after the *halt ! drefs !* gives time in large fronts for exact dreffing, before the *march !* is refumed; yet in fmall ones, where that paufe is fhort, there is no time for fuch operation : the atten- tion to, and prefervation of the true diftance, being then the material object. Whenever the wheel made is lefs than the quarter circle, the paufe after the wheel will be confiderable; fhould the wheel be greater than the quarter circle, it muft be accelerated, otherwife more than one divifion will be arrived and arrefted at the wheeling point.

On a
moveable
pivot.

When wheels or changes of direction of bodies in column, are made on a MOVEABLE PIVOT, both flanks are kept in motion, the *pivot* one always defcribing part of a circle, and the *reverfe* flank, and intermediate men of the divifion, by a compound of inclining and wheel- ing, conforming to the pivot movement.

S. 6. Filing.

Filings.

FILING is an operation of the fquadron, of ufe in broken or embarraffed ground, which will not allow of movements on a greater front. It is a fituation in which horfes move free and without confinement, but in which the fquadron or its parts lengthen out, and take up much more ground than what they ftand on in line; and is therefore to be had recourfe to only from neceffity.

Attentions
in filing.

All horfes heads are inftantly to be turned at the command to *File !* ready to move off without lofs of diftance. The leaders of files go off fhort and quick, in their ordered direction, and are followed clofe by each man as it comes to his turn, fo as to leave no unneccef- fary interval from one to another, and inftantly to get off the ground. After being once in file, a diftance of a yard from head to tail may be taken, fo as to trot or gallop the eafier if required. Every alteration of pace ought to be made as much as poffible, by the whole at once;

once; if this is not obferved, a crowding and ftop in the rear will always attend fuch alteration.

The file leaders preferve fuch diftances as they ought, from which ever hand they are to drefs to, and the followers of each file are only attentive to cover, and be regulated by their proper file leaders. In file, the rear rank dreffes by, and is regulated by its front rank.

Diftances when in file.

In forming, each man muft come up in file to his place, and by no means move up to his leader, till that leader has formed to which ever hand the file is forming to. The whole muft follow the exact tract of the firft leader, and come up one by one into their refpective places in fquadron.

Attentions in forming.

Filings that may be required from the fquadron, are filing from either or both flanks, to front, flank, or rear, filing from the center of the fquadron to the front or to the flank. Filing fingle men by ranks, or by front and rear rank men alternately, from either flank of the fquadron.

General and neceffary filing.

In the filings of the fquadron, the ferrefiles take their place in the rear of the files, unlefs the ground will allow them to remain on the flank of the rear rank; but their general and proper pofition, is in the rear of the files, becaufe filing is in general an operation of neceffity, which the nature of the ground requires.

Serrefiles in filing.

S. 7. Inclining.

INCLINING is a movement, by which the fquadron is carried on in a parallel direction, at the fame time that it is gaining ground to the flank. It is of great ufe in the marching of the line in front, to correct any irregularities that may happen : it is equivalent to the oblique marching of the infantry. It enables to gain the enemy's flank, without expofing your own, or without wheeling or altering the parallel front of the fquadron.

Inclining.

At the word to INCLINE ! each man makes a half face on

on his horfe's fore feet, by which means, each will appear to be half a head behind his flank leader; and the whole will look to the hand to which they are to incline.

The leading officer on the flank, with a glance of his eye, afcertaining his points, marches fteadily upon them, at whatever pace is ordered. Every other man in the fquadron moves in fo many parallel lines, with refpect to him, and preferves the fame uniformity of front and file, as when he firft turned his horfe's head.

At no time of the incline, ought the former front of the fquadron, or diftance of files, to be altered. But whenever the word FRONT! is given, the fquadron (by each man at the fame inftant turning his horfe) fhould be formed in a direction perfectly parallel to its former front, and ready to drefs and move on by its ftandard.

The diftance of files, at fix inches, allows the fquadron to incline in perfect order, while its new direction does not pafs an angle of thirty-four degrees, with refpect to its former one; and at this angle it will be underftood always to incline; unlefs it fhould be required to gain as much or more ground to the flank, as to the front: in that cafe the fquadron muft either wheel up, and march upon the flank point, or it will fall more or lefs into file, according to the degree of obliquity required, by moving each horfe retired half neck, or head to boot.

S. 8. Pace.

THE *Walk! Trot!* and *Gallop!* are the three natural paces, and of each of thefe there are different degrees of quicknefs; but at which ever of them the fquadron is conducted, the floweft moving horfe at that pace muft be attended to, otherwife different kinds of motions will exift at the fame time in the fquadron, and tend to difunite it.

All alterations of pace muft be made as much as poffible

poffible at the fame inftant, by each feparate body that compofes a line or column.

Though in flow movements of the line or fquadron, and on a march, the *Walk !* is the common pace ufed; yet in general, all changes of pofition and manœuvres, fhould be made at the *Trot !* or *Gallop !* according to circumftances, beginning gently to avoid hurry, and ending gently to avoid confufion in forming.

The intermediate times of fuch movement may be conducted with rapidity, and much depends on the eye of the officer, and well-timing the words of command.

S. 9. *Of the Charge or Attack.*

THE great force of cavalry is more in the offenfive than the defenfive, therefore the attack is its principal object. All the different movements of the fquadron fhould tend to place it in the moft advantageous fituation to attack the enemy.

The charge is that attack made with the greateft rapidity and regularity poffible, to break the order of the oppofite enemy, which will always enfure his defeat.

When the fquadron is to charge, the leader gives the words of command, MARCH! TROT! GALLOP! CHARGE! HALT! DRESS!

It depends on the commanding officer to lead at fuch a pace, as that the flanks and rear rank may always keep up. Every alteration of pace muft be made at the fame inftant by the whole fquadron.

Whatever diftance the fquadron has to go over, it may move at a brifk trot, till within two hundred and fifty yards of the enemy, and then gallop. The word CHARGE ! is given, when within eighty yards, and the gallop increafed as much as the body can bear in good order. Any attempt to clofe the files, at the inftant of the charge, would only increafe the intervals in a line,

line, and tend to impede the free movement of each horfe, who at no time requires to be more independent than when galloping at his utmoft exertion, and every rub to right or left diminifhes that effort in a degree.

At the inftant of the fhock, the body muft be well back, the horfe not reftrained by the bit, but determined forward by the fpur; rifing in the ftirrups and pointing the fword, will always occafion a fhake in the fquadron; it will naturally be done when neceffary.

It is in the uniform velocity of the fquadron its effects confift; the fpur as much as the fword tends to overfet an oppofite enemy; when the one has nearly accomplifhed this end, the other may complete it.

In every part of the charge and in quick movement, the ftandard muft be very exact in following the leader, and the men particularly attentive in keeping up to, and dreffing to their ftandard.

When the fhock of the fquadron has broken the order of the oppofite enemy, part may be ordered to purfue and keep up the advantage, but its great object is inftantly to rally, and to renew its efforts in a body, either to the front, or by wheeling to take other fquadrons in flank.

A fquadron fhould never be fo much hurried, as to bring up the horfes blown to the charge, and this will much depend on circumftances and the order they are in.

The regiment and fquadrons muft be well dreffed before they move, horfes perfectly ftraight, and carried on fo during the whole of the attack, files on no account crowding; paces even and determined, horfes in hand, and perfect attention and fteadinefs of every individual.

S. 10. *Commands.*

Command and duty of officers.

All COMMANDS muft be given by officers, firm, loud, and explicit; every officer muft therefore be accuftomed to give fuch commands, even to the fmalleft bodies, in

the

the full extent of his voice. By fuch bodies he muft not only be heard, but by the leaders of others who are dependent on his motions. The juftnefs of execution and confidence of the foldier can only be in proportion to the firm, decided, and proper manner in which every officer of every rank gives his orders.

Commands of CAUTION, being fuch as are preparatory to a movement, fhould be fufficiently full and explanatory. Commands of EXECUTION fhould be fhort, and avoiding uneffential words.

Nature of commands

The commanding officers of regiments give and repeat all general commands, which are alfo fhortly and quickly repeated by commanding officers of fquadrons, efpecially fuch as MARCH ! HALT ! DRESS ! It is only when the fquadrons and line are broken into parts that the divifion officers give commands, and thofe chiefly executory, as HALT ! DRESS ! &c. alfo the feveral words neceffary for the wheels made in column of march by each divifion, the feveral words neceffary when the divifions come up fucceffively from open or clofe column into line or column, whether conducted by line or flank movements, and in general whenever their divifions are moving as diftinct though dependent bodies. But the wheeling from column into general line, or from line into general column, is made at the word MARCH ! repeated by leaders of fquadrons; the whole column is alfo put in march and halted by word from the leaders of fquadrons, as is the fquadron and regiment in all movements of the line in front.

Commands given by refpective leaders.

It is impoffible to afcertain the words of command to be given in all cafes; where fuch are not pointed out they muft depend on the circumftances of the fituation, and be fhort, clear, and expreffive of what is to be done.

All commands cannot be afcertained.

When a general order is not heard by a part of the line, each regimental commander (when the intention is obvious) will conform as quickly as poffible to the movement which he fees executed on his right or left, according to the point from whence he perceives it to begin—but fquadron and divifion officers execute only on the orders of their regimental commander.

When commands are not diftinctly heard.

After

After the chief commander has announced the orders,
and particularly the words of execution, as MARCH!
FORM! HALT! &c. the repetition of them by every
other individual concerned muft not be ftrictly fucceffive, but as much as can be in a volley, to beget that
precifion of movement which in manœuvre is indifpen-
fible; and the larger the body, the more effentially does
this circumftance operate.

In the quick movements and manœuvres of cavalry
there is not time for the full and formal words of command, on fuch occafions they muft be rapidly given,
much abridged, and all expletives omitted.

S. 11. *Movements.*

MOVEMENTS muft be divided into diftinct parts, and
each executed by feparate and explanatory words of
command.

Alterations of pofition, in confiderable bodies, muft
begin from a previous HALT! however fhort; except
giving a new direction to the heads of columns, or encreafing or diminifhing their fronts, which may be
done while in motion. As the principle of moving,
forming, and dreffing, upon given and determined
points is juft, quick changes of pofition of a confiderable
body, formed in line, attempted while on the move, and
not proceeding from a previous halt (however fhort)
will be falfe and defective; the effects of which, though
not fo apparent in a fingle fquadron or regiment, would
be very obvious in a line or column of any extent. A
paufe between each change of fituation, fo effentially
neceffary to the movements of great bodies, fhould feldom be omitted in thofe of fmall ones; fquarenefs of
dreffing, the exact perpendiculars of march, and the correct relative pofition of the whole are thereby afcertained. Such alterations of fituation made from the halt
may, when neceffary, fucceed each other inftantly and
quickly; no time need be taken up in fcrupulous dreffing,

fing, but every one may be immediately apprized of the following movement which circumftances require.

In the movements of a SINGLE Regiment, and in the taking up of a new pofition, it may not feem material whether a flank of it is placed a few yards to the one hand or other, or whether the line formed on is exactly directed on any certain point.—But when a regiment makes a part of a more confiderable body, then all its pofitions being relative to other regiments and to given points, if its formations are not accurate and juft, it will create general confufion, and give falfe directions and diftances to thofe whofe fituations may be determined by it.

Neceffity of precifion in the movements of fingle regiments.

The neceffity of every fingle regiment being accuftomed to make its changes of pofition and formation on determined points, is therefore obvious, and to which they fhould be carefully trained.

If OFFICERS are obferving of, and attentive to their true diftances of divifions, and of the covering of their pivot flanks, the moft confiderable column of cavalry ought to be able in changing its pofition, to ENTER on a given alignement, at a brifk TROT;—To HALT !— To WHEEL INTO LINE !—To ADVANCE !—And to CHARGE !—without more than a momentary paufe between each operation of the halt, wheel and advance, and without being under any neceffity of dreffing, correcting diftances, or alteration whatever.

What is required of a line of cavalry.

Although the nature of Routes and of Roads may fometimes limit common marches to be made on a very fmall front, yet flank marches near an enemy, or changes of pofition in the prefence of an enemy, cannot be effected with precifion, firmnefs, or certainty, on a lefs front than *ranks by threes*, or indeed when poffible on a front of a *divifion* (or of a *fub-divifion*, if the fquadron is ftrong as from forty eight to fixty files) for then the fteadinefs and correctnefs of pivot officers may enfure the inftant HALT !—WHEEL INTO LINE !—and ADVANCE !—upon the enemy.—And it will feldom
happen

Movements in column if poffible to be made by divifions or fub-divifions.

happen that changes of pofition made in order to attack to the greater advantage will be required; but in fituations that allow fuch changes to be made by a flank movement, and without lengthening out the line during the tranfition from one point to another.

S. 12. *Line of March and Formation.*

Movements in a ftraight line always made on two objects

Every LEADER of a body, moving on any front whatever, who means to conduct it in a ftraight line, muft march upon *two* points, which he invariably preferves fo as to cover each other; if fuch points are not afcertained for him he muft inftantly determine them for himfelf, and if no ftrong or marked objects prefent themfelves in his direction, he can never fail by cafting his eyes along the ground, to find fuch fmall ones as will anfwer his purpofe, and thefe from time to time he renews as he approaches them.—To march ftraight on one object only with certainty and without wavering is not to be depended on.

The alignement

To march or form in the *alignement*, is to make troops march and form in any part of the ftraight line which joins two given points, or is prolonged beyond them.

Taking up a line of formation.

The *line* on which troops in column move ftraight, or on which they are fucceffively to form, is taken up to an extent by the prolongation of an original, fhort, and given *bafe* of two perfons placed where the troops begin firft to enter, or form upon that line ; the direction of which has been determined by the views of the commander, and which can feldom fail to point on fome diftant and diftinct object, that will ferve to correct the pofition of the different perfons who fucceffively, as their feparate bodies require it, prolong the line from the feveral points already eftablifhed in it.

Pofition of markers of the line.

When the leading body of a column arrives at any point where it is to enter on a ftraight line, a perfon will be placed with his horfe's head facing to the pivot flank

of

of the column; each leader will thus know why he is fo placed, and will, in pafling clofe to him and to every other perfon pofted in a fimilar manner, give every attention to continue the alignement.

Afcertaining the points neceffary for the movements and formations of the regiment, is the particular bufinefs of the adjutant in the field; in this exercife he may be affifted by detached perfons placed behind each flank, who are properly trained quickly to take up fuch line as he fhall give them; and for this purpofe they are only to be fent out fucceffively, and as their aid is wanted, nor are they to make any buftle or unneceffary parade; and when the operation for which they are fent out is accomplifhed, they will return immediately behind their proper flank.

Points of movement and formation afcertained by appointed perfons.

The neceffity of officers and non-commiffioned officers being well trained, to prolong lines, take up diftances, and give thofe aids which are fo effential in the formations and movements of all confiderable bodies, is evident, and much to be attended to. Perfons active, intelligent, and well mounted, can alone affift the operations of cavalry, nor are camp colours, nor any fuch improper and fuperfluous modes neceffary, or in general to be ufed.

The neceffity of perfons well trained to prolong and give line of march and formation.

The markers of the alignement in column, or of the formations in line, are not to quit their ground after the halt of either, till all neceffary dreffing is accomplifhed, and that they are directed fo to do; they ferve not only as points of movement, but as points of correction.

S. 13. *Breaking and forming Squadrons.*

When the fquadron has wheeled to a flank by *half fquadrons*, by *divifions*, or by *fvb-divifions* of more than fix files, it then occupies lefs ground than it before ftood on, by the front of the column, whatever it is.

Whenever

<table>
<tr>
<td>Leaders of divifions of the fquadron.</td>
<td>Whenever the Squadron is broken into divifions, or parts, for the purpofe of movement, each feparate body has a leader, on whom the eye and attention of each foldier is fixed. In column fuch leader will be on the pivot flank of his divifion in all fituations of manœuvre. Thefe leaders cover each other in the given direction in which the column is to move; they are not themfelves then to be covered by any one, and are anfwerable for true diftances. Should any fuch leader not be appointed, or be wanting to a divifion, his place is to remain vacant, and not to be occupied by the flank files of men, for fuch flank files of men are invariably to remain covering each other.</td>
</tr>
</table>

Leaders of divifions of the fqua-dron.

Whenever the Squadron is broken into divifions, or parts, for the purpofe of movement, each feparate body has a leader, on whom the eye and attention of each foldier is fixed. In *column* fuch leader will be on the pivot flank of his divifion in all fituations of manœuvre. Thefe leaders cover each other in the given direction in which the column is to move; they are not themfelves then to be covered by any one, and are anfwerable for true diftances. Should any fuch leader not be appointed, or be wanting to a divifion, his place is to remain vacant, and not to be occupied by the flank files of men, for fuch flank files of men are invariably to remain covering each other.

Commands given when the fqua-dronbreaks to a flank by any of its tellings off.

When from the halt, the fquadron, by wheels to its flank, *breaks into open column*, the commanding officer gives the words (HALF SQUADRONS, DIVISIONS, SUB-DIVISIONS) TO THE $\left\{ \begin{array}{c} \text{Right} \\ \text{or} \\ \text{Left} \end{array} \right\}$ WHEEL! MARCH! HALT! DRESS! by the ftanding flank, and then EYES $\left\{ \begin{array}{c} \text{Right} \\ \text{or} \\ \text{Left} \end{array} \right\}$ by the pivot flank; after which the whole is put in motion by the word MARCH! Should the word EYES (right or left) be omitted, at any rate they are directed to the pivot flank, at the word MARCH!

Pivot lead-ers in co-lumn of half fqua-drons.

When the fquadron has wheeled to a flank by *half fquadrons. If to the right,* the officer from the right of the fquadron immediately fhifts to the left of his half fquadron, to conduct the pivot of the leading half fqua-dron, and the officer who was on the left of the fquadron wheels up, and remains on the pivot of his own half fquadron. *If to the left,* then the left officer fhifts to the right of his half fquadron, and the right offi-cer wheels up, and remains on the right of his own half fquadron.

Standard in column.

In the wheelings of the fquadron into *half fquadrons, divifions,* or *fub-divifions,* the ftandard and its coverer wheel up with the leading half fquadron, or the fecond divifion, or the fourth fub-divifion from the flank wheeled to, to, fo as to place themfelves, at the conclufion of the wheel, behind the fecond and third file from the pivot of each of the faid bodies. And when thefe bodies wheel up to form fquadron, the ftandard fhifts brifkly to its place in the center during the wheel.

When from the halt the fquadron wheels to its flank, *ranks by three's* or *by two's*, the commanding officer gives the words (Ranks by Three's or by Two's)

to the Right or Left Wheel! March! Halt! Dress!

to the pivot hand, after which the whole is put in motion at the fecond word March! the whole three's at the fame time, and increafing their diftances while on the move; or the two's (who are ftanding at a half wheel) fucceffively, as foon as each is enabled fo to do, and can get its marching diftance.

Commands given when a fquadron wheels to a flank ranks by three's or by two's.

When the fquadron wheels to the right or left, by *ranks by three's*, the middle man of each three will turn on his horfe's fore feet; and of the other two, one will rein back, and the other moves forward to drefs with him. A flank officer is at the head of the fquadron, the other flank officer at the rear. The ftandard is in the middle of the leading center rank of fixes when wheeled up, and its coverer is in the middle of the rank behind it. The fupernumeraries of the rear rank will, if the ground requires it, fall in and follow the rear of the fquadron, or otherwife turn fingly, and march on its flank. In this fituation in movement, the fquadron has opened out one fixth more than the ground it ftood formed on.

Column of ranks by three's.

When the fquadron wheels to a flank, by *ranks by two's*, the flank man of each two will half turn on his horfe's fore feet, and the other man will half wheel up, fo as to make a half face to the flank, and be in a fituation to move off fucceffively as it comes to their turn. A flank officer is at the head of the fquadron, the other flank officer in the rear of it. The ftandard and its coverer turn each on his own ground, and move between the ranks; the ferrefiles of the rear will, if the ground requires it, fall in and follow the rear of the fquadron,

Column of ranks by two's.

C   or

or otherwise turn singly, and march on its flank. In this situation in movement, the squadron has opened out near two thirds more than the ground it stood formed on.

Serrefiles in column. When, for the purpose of *manœuvre*, the squadron breaks to the flank by half squadrons or divisions, the serrefiles are close up behind each; when by sub-divisions, they are on the flank, not the pivot one.

Halts of divisions. *Halts* of divisions from wheels, are made with eyes turned to the standing flank.

Post of commanding officers. Commanding officers of regiments and squadrons remain on (but wide of) the pivot flanks, to observe and regulate the march, and instantaneously to form when ordered.

Shifting of officers to pivot flanks. Commanding officers must take care that conducting officers of flanks or pivots shift nimbly to such points, at the proper instant they should there place themselves.

Formation of the squadron and line from column of divisions. If a line has marched to a flank in *column of squadrons, half squadrons, divisions,* or *sub-divisions,* in such cases it occupies (intervals being preserved) exactly the ground requisite for its formation in line; which is at any instant made by halting, and wheeling up the quarter circle.

Formation of the squadron and line from column of ranks by three's. If a line is moving to a flank, squadrons by *ranks by three's.* As each squadron in march then occupies more ground than what it stands on when formed, and that about half the intervals still ought to remain, therefore if the whole halts at the same instant, and *each* squadron wheels up its three's closing them at the same time to its leading flank, the line should then be completely formed with its proper interval. The squadrons thus forming all at the same time.

Formation of the squadron and line from column of ranks by two's. If a line is marching correctly to the flank, *ranks by two's,* every man as close as he well can to his preceding file leader, no distance between squadrons, that it halts, and that the pivot men are covered, such line will still have lengthened out considerably, viz. one third at least. Therefore, if it forms to the pivot flank, the four leading men of the head squadron wheel up to the flank by two's;

two's; the other men of the leading fquadron fuccef-fively wheel up when they clofe to their refpective lead-ers; each other fquadron, as its head arrives at its in-terval diftance from the preceding one, halts and forms in the fame manner. The fquadrons thus form fuccef-fively as they gain their diftances.

When from the halt, and from open column, the fquadron is formed by the *wheeling up of its divifions.* The commanding officer gives the words (Half Squa-drons, Divifions, Sub-Divifions, Ranks by Three's) WHEEL INTO LINE! on which pivot leaders imme-diately place themfelves on the reverfe flank of fuch divifion, as by its wheel up brings them to their true place in the fquadron; the pivot officer of the rear di-vifion is alone an exception, being already at his poft in fquadron. At the word MARCH! the whole wheel up, and receive the word HALT! DRESS! by the ftanding flank, and the line of pivots; the ftandard, ferrefiles, and every thing having refumed their place in fquadron. Squadrons forming from ranks by *two's,* receive fuccef-fively from their leaders, as their heads come to their ground, the words, WHEEL INTO SQUADRON! HALT; DRESS! to the hand formed to.

When the column of — wheels up into fquadron or line.

In wheeling from column into line, it is on the *flank files of men,* and not on the pivot leaders that the wheels are made; therefore, at the word being given to WHEEL INTO LINE! thofe leaders quit the flanks, and are dif-pofed of as above, and this allows that after the wheel the horfes heads of the pivot men exactly touch the heads of thofe that are facing towards and marking the general line.

Wheels from co-lumn into line made on pivot files of men.

When the open column of fquadrons ftands halted, ready to *wheel up into line,* on the caution fo to do, and before the word MARCH! an officer or under officer from the wheeling flank (or from the rear) of each fquadron, moves quickly forward, and places himfelf in the line of pivots, and thereby becomes an object, which determines the fquare of the wheel, and which the out-ward man of each fquadron knows he is not to pafs. In an open column of half fquadrons, the leading half only of each fquadron will fend out fuch an object, as

Aids ne-ceffary to be given when the column moves up into line.

C 2

the

the rear half (if diſtances are juſt) wheels up to the pivot of the leading half. In an open column of diviſions, or ſub-diviſions, the leading one of each will only ſend out ſuch object. In column of ranks by three's, or by two's, commanding officers of regiments will always endeavour by detached perſons, to prolong the line as taken from the head of the column, in order to make their re-ſpective formations correct in the general line. The rear diviſion of a column, before it wheels up into line, will always place an object of formation behind its pivot flank, and ſuch object is the one on which the flank ſquadron is corrected after the wheel into line.

S. 14. *Open Column.*

Formation of columns

ALL COLUMNS are ſuppoſed formed from line, for the convenience of movement, and for the purpoſe of again extending into line. Every column of march or manœuvre muſt be formed by a regular ſucceſſion of the diviſions from one flank to the other of the line, or of ſuch of its parts as compoſe the column, for whatever is the relative poſition of a body in line, ſuch ought it to be in column; and where ſeveral connected columns are formed, the ſame flanks of each ſhould be in front ; but whether rights or lefts will depend on circumſtances. Columns formed from the center of regiments or lines will ſeldom be made, are partial, and not adapted as the others are to movements, and formations in all ſitua-tions.

Columns of march and ma-nœuvre.

The column is named that of *march*, or *route*, when applied to common marches, where the attention of men and officers is not ſo much kept on the ſtretch. It is named the *column of manœuvre*, when being within reach of an enemy, the greateſt exactneſs is required, in order to its ſpeedy formation at any inſtant into line during its tranſition from one poſition to another.

Front and extent of columns.

Columns of march or manœuvre will be compoſed of diviſions, ſub-diviſions, or ranks by three's ; for the purpoſes of movement they need not exceed twelve file
in

in front, nor fhould they be under fix men in front, otherwife there will not be fpace to loofen the ranks, and the line will be of courfe lengthened out, as happens in the march of ranks by two's or by files. From fix to ten men in front are moft advantageoufly compofed for quick manœuvres.

Columns of march or manœuvre will be formed with the left in front, whenever it is probable that the formation of the line will be required to the right flank, and *vice verfa* when required to the left flank.

Circum-
ftances de-
termine the
leading
flank of co-
lumns.

The proper pivot flank in column, is that which, when wheeled up to, preferves the divifions of the line in the natural order, and to their proper front; the other may be called the *reverfe flank.* In column, divifions cover and drefs to the proper pivot flank; to the left when the right is in front, and to the right when the left is in front.

Pivot flank
and reverfe
flank of di-
vifions, &c.
in column.

In column the chief commander is with the leading divifion, and in line with the directing fquadron.

In all movements, formations, and changes of pofition of the column, *diftances and dreffing* are taken from the directing hand, viz. from the head of the column, or from the hand to which the formation is making, or to be made.

Diftances
and dref-
fing where
taken from.

In column, the *pivot officers*, or non-commiffioned officers, are anfwerable for covering, and for proper wheeling diftances, and the eyes of the whole are turned to the pivot; fuch pivot leaders muft attend to thofe two circumftances only, and by no means be looking to or giving directions to their divifions; that care muft be left to the officers on the other flank, or in the rear; for if they themfelves move fteadily and truly, there is little doubt but their divifions will always keep up to them.

Pivot Offi-
cers.

The rear divifions of a column in march always follow every turn and twift which the head makes; each fucceffively changing its direction at whatever point the leading one may have fo done. When at an unexpected moment a column is ordered to halt, the pivot leaders of

Attention
of the rear
divifions of
the column
when in
march.

C 3   each

each divifiou muft remain fixed where they are found, at the word HALT. If the march of the column is again to be refumed, the rear divifions will continue to follow the exact path traced out by the head; nor are any of the following divifions of a column ever to deviate from this rule, or endeavour of themfelves to get into a ftraight line, when the general direction is a winding one, until an exprefs order is given for that purpofe, which can hardly ever happen, till the head of the column is halted, with a determination to form the line in a ftraight direction, in which cafe the correction of pivots will begin from the head of the column.

Commander and Adjutant of a regiment correct pivots. *In column, the commander* of a regiment remains near its leading divifion, and the adjutant (or fome appointed perfon) remains near its clofing divifion; they are thus ready to preferve the line of march, and at the inftant of halting, to make fuch correction of pivots as may be neceffary; for which purpofe the adjutant takes care immediately to place himfelf in the prolongation of the general line, which he takes up from the points in his front already eftablifhed in it, and from fuch bodies as before him have already halted in it. In this manner the adjutant in his own perfon gives the flank point on which each commander from his leading divifion at all times forms and dreffes his fquadron and regiment.

The front of column not to be altered when marching in an alignement *No doubling up,* encreafing, or diminifhing the front of the Column, muft be made after entering on a ftraight alignement in order to form in line; fuch operation, when neceffary, fhould be performed before the line of formation is entered on.

***

Correction of pivots of open column before wheeling into line. *When the open column* has marched on in an alignement, and is ordered to halt and form line, the pivots of the leading regiment are immediately corrected if neceffary, the others inftantly perfect their line upon it, and upon each other, and no time is loft in wheeling up into line and then advancing.

Correction of the fquadron and of the line af- *If the regiment,* after wheeling up from column into line, is not critically well dreffed, the fault muft be in the internal part of the divifions; this muft be immediately

diately corrected by each fquadron leader on his former pivot men, who on no account muft have moved; but remain fo many fixed points, on whom the whole are lined. If any farther dreffing is neceffary, it is ordered and made by a field officer, who himfelf moves quickly clofe along the front from the flank to which eyes are turned, to the other flank.

ter wheel-ingup from a column.

A column in movement fhould, if poffible, never occupy more ground than what it ftands on in line: but when the formation into line muft undoubtedly be to the front, then the divifions may be ordered to march clofed up to half, quarter, or any other diftance, and the formation may be made by prolonging the line, by deployment, by inclining up, or by half wheels, and marching in the oblique lines, as circumftances require.

Neceffary extent of a column of march.

Columns marching at half or quarter diftance of their then front muft alfo make their neceffary wheels on a *moveable* pivot, otherwife a ftop muft enfue, and a column open out.

In all wheels of a column, in movement to change direction, and made by divifions on a *fixed* flank, the outward file, whether officer or man, is the one wheeled upon; and the quicknefs of the wheels muft at leaft be double to the rate of march, otherwife the column may be liable to open out, and the wheeling point would not be cleared in time for each fucceffive divifion. In changes made on a *moveable* flank, the outward file of that flank is alfo the directing one.

Quicknefs of wheels in column.

Halts of divifions from wheels are made with eyes turned to the ftanding flank. But all *halts* from a march in front are made with the eyes turned to the point or points to which the troops while in march are looking. After which, no dreffing or movement whatever is to be made, until a feparate order directs it.

Halting from the wheel or from march.

The whole column or line fhould always be in fo correct a fituation, as to halt inftantly on the word HALT!

The halt of the line or column.

But

But fhould, at any time, the difficulties of the ground have unavoidably opened out the column, or thrown fquadrons out of the line, in fuch cafe the halt of thofe fquadrons will be fucceffive, as they regain their proper fituations.

Deployments, &c. made by ranks by three's. *When fquadrons,* half fquadrons, or divifions, feparately move by a flank, to change pofition in column, or from line to place themfelves in open or clofe column, or from clofe column to deploy into line, &c. it will always, when poffible, be done by *ranks by three's,* and the greateft care be given, that the three's move as clofe as they can, that at the inftant the word HALT! FRONT! is given to each, the divifion may be exactly formed by the wheeling of its three's, without any neceffity of a clofing in of its rear.

Poft of commanding officers of each regiment. *The commanding officers* of regiments are in the charge at the head of one of their fquadrons, generally of the one neareft that of direction. In all other fituations of manœuvre they are moveable according to circumftances, in general near the head of their column, or of their body, which firft forms in line; when the line is formed in parade, they are at the head of their right fquadron.

CHANGES OF POSITION OF A REGIMENT.

OPEN COLUMN.

S. 15. *When the Open Column wheels on its halted reverfe Flank into a new Alignement, and marches on it.*

CAUTION TO

⎧ The new alignement being determined by placed objects, and the point of entry being marked, the leading officer who has marched his ⎫

	his pivot flank on that point, when he arrives at a diftance equal to the front of his divifion from it, orders
Right wheel!	(right or left) *wheel!* (according to whatever is the reverfe flank) ; and the wheel is made fo that on the conclufion of it, at the word,
Halt, Drefs!	*Halt, Drefs!* he himfelf fhall be placed on the new alignement on the pivot of his divifion, ready to
March!	give the word *March!* as foon as the fucceeding divifion has arrived at the wheeling point.

	The officer of the Second divifion gives the word *Wheel!* when
Wheel!	he arrives at the ground which the
Halt, Drefs!	firft is quitting, and then *Halt! Drefs!* when the wheel is completed; in this fituation he remains till he perceives the preceding divifion has gained from him a diftance equal to the front of his divifion, he then inftantly gives
March!	the word *March!* and follows in column. Each fucceeding divifion obferves the fame directions, and the equality of pace being preferved, the column may continue its march in perfect order.

‗‗‗‗‗‗

S. 16. *When the Open Column wheels on its halted pivot Flank into a new Alignement, and marches in it.*

CAUTION.	The leading divifion begins its wheel to the pivot flank on the
Left, Wheel!	alignement itfelf, when its pivot
Halt, Drefs!	flank officer arrives at the point of wheeling

March !	wheeling, inftead of (as in the preceding fection) beginning at the diftance of a divifion fhort of that point.

S. 17. When Part of the Open Column halts in the new Direction, and the remaining Divifions are ordered to enter by flank Marching.

Halt !	When the head of a regimental column arrives at a given point, the whole is ordered to Halt ! Such divifions of the column as are ftill in the old direction are
Three's, Right wheel ! March ! *Halt, Drefs !* March ! *Halt,—Wheel up !* *Halt, Drefs !*	then ordered to Wheel to their pivot flank ranks by three's—They March ! and fucceffively place their pivots on the new line at their juft wheeling diftances, which are afcertained for them by the perfons they timeoufly detach for that purpofe. The whole pivots being thus covered and dreffed in the new direction, the column is prepared for wheeling into line.

ON A FIXED POINT.

S. 18. When the Regiment forms Open Column of Divifions behind a placed Flank Divifion, and throws back the other Flank.

Two perfons are advanced immediately before the flank divifion to mark, and who face to the determined line on which the pivots of the column are to ftand.

The

CAUTION.

{ The flank divifion is *placed* perpendicular to that line, and with its pivot upon it.

DIVISIONS,
RIGHT WHEEL!
MARCH!
HALT, DRESS!

} The line WHEELS up into open column of fimilar divifions, towards the placed divifion.

THREE's,
RIGHT WHEEL!
MARCH!
HALT, DRESS!

{ The divifions having wheeled the quarter circle, each breaks ranks by three's, the reverfe and not the pivot flank leading, and the conductor being there placed.

MARCH!
Halt! Wheel up!
Halt, Drefs!

{ The divifions MARCH! and form in open column behind the head divifion and each other, preferving their wheeling and interval diftances, and placing their pivot flanks on the new line, which is taken from the original objects in it, and prolonged to each of them by their own detached perfons. The *pivots* being covered and dreffed, and diftances juft from front to rear of the column, the whole is in a fituation to *wheel* into line.

{ The better to afcertain thofe flank points, the coverer of each pivot leader will fucceffively, as they approach the new line, gallop on and place himfelf upon it at the wheeling diftance of his divifion from the one before him, facing to the head of the column, and covering exactly thofe that have already taken their places therein —The coverer thus ftanding on the fpot which his leader is afterwards to occupy, fuch and every other leader, when he arrives

Halt! Wheel up!
Halt, Drefs!

rives at the line, ftops there himfelf, allows his divifion to pafs on
behind its marker, till its *rear*
comes up ; he then *Halts, Fronts*
it, and *dreffes* and clofes it to its
pivot marker on the line. It is
to be obferved, that in this cafe
the divifions *crofs* the new line,
in order to place their pivots
upon it.

All divifions that by flank marching mean to form
in open column on a new line, fhould take particular
care that the laft part of their movements, and at leaft
for a fpace equal to their own extent, is made in a line
not oblique, but fquare and perpendicular to the line
of pivots, for thereby they will at once form up firm,
compact, and on their true ground; and therefore in
the firft part of their march, the head of their divifions
fhould not be directed on their future pivot point, but
rather wide of it, fo as to allow for the fquare entry of
each on its forming ground.

If when from line, divifions wheel into open column
towards a ftanding divifion, and the flanks of the divifion next fuch ftanding one may not thereby be fufficiently difengaged for whatever movement is immediately to be required, fuch divifion (alone) may be ordered only to half wheel, quarter wheel, or rein back
a flank, as may beft anfwer the propofed end.

S. 19. *When the Regiment forms Open Column of Divifions before a Flank Divi-fion, and throws forward the other Flank.*

Two perfons are placed behind the flank divifion, in
order to give the determined line on which the pivots
of the column are to ftand, as directed in the preceding
movement.

The

CAUTION.	The *flank* divifion by wheeling, or countermarching, is placed with its pivot on, and perpendicular to that line, and in fuch fituation it makes front towards the rear.
DIVISIONS, RIGHT WHEEL! MARCH! HALT, DRESS!	The line wheels up into open column of divifions towards the placed divifion.
THREE'S, LEFT WHEEL! MARCH! *Halt, Drefs!*	The divifions having wheeled the quarter circle, each goes ranks by three's, the pivot flank leading.
MARCH! *Halt! Wheel up! Halt, Drefs!*	The divifions MARCH and form open column as, before—In this cafe, as their pivot flanks lead, they do not *crofs* the new line, but arrive at and place them upon it; the pivot leader himfelf there remaining. The pivots being covered and diftances juft, the column ftands ready to WHEEL into line, or to march on.

S. 20. *When the Regiment forms open Column of Divifions, before and behind a central Divifion.*

The *central* divifion is named, and alfo the wings, as they are to be before or behind it.

The *new* direction is taken, and the central divifion placed.

CAUTION! DIVISIONS WHEEL INWARDS! MARCH! HALT, DRESS!	The line is ordered to WHEEL inwards by divifions of fquadron towards the placed divifion, and thus ftands in two open columns facing each other.

The

THREE'S, RIGHT WHEEL!	The divisions WHEEL ranks by threes, both to the same flank, viz. their leading one, which in those that are to move to the front is the *pivot* flank, and in those that are to move to the rear, is the *reverse* flank.
MARCH! *Halt, Dress!* MARCH!	
HALT! WHEEL UP! *Halt, Dress !*	The part of the line, which leads with its reverse flank, forms in column *behind* the placed division, the part which leads with its pivot flank forms in column *before* the placed division; and its head division is to remember, that if the line is afterwards to be formed, it will take a double wheeling distance from the division it fronts, as they would then wheel up towards each other; but if the column is to move on, it will take only single distance.

In this formation the *pivot* line should be sufficiently marked by detached persons, both before and behind the central division, and the pivots of the wing, which forms behind it, will take their general direction from the pivots of those that form before it, as these last have the greatest facility in forming in consequence of their pivot flanks leading.

When the *whole* are thus in column, facing the central division, if the line is to be formed, the whole will WHEEL up to their pivots—If the column is to march, the necessary part of it will COUNTERMARCH its divisions, and then the whole can move on.

S. 21. *When the Regiment changes to a diſtant Poſition in Front or Rear, by the Flank marching of the open Column, and that this Poſition is either parallel or oblique to the one it quits.*

DIVISIONS—
WHEEL! MARCH!
HALT, DRESS!

{ The regiment breaks into open column of diviſions to whichever hand the new poſition out-flanks the old one, for to that hand will the whole have to incline during the march; and if it does not ſenſibly out-flank, then the regiment will break to the hand next to the point of interſection of the two lines, for that hand is neareſt to, and will, in general, be the firſt to enter any part of the new poſition.

THREES—WHEEL!
MARCH!
Halt, Dreſs!

{ The regiment ſtanding in open column is ordered to WHEEL its diviſions by *three's* to a flank. The leader of the ſecond diviſion has then a direction given him, which croſſes the new line at the point, as near as can be judged, where the flank of that diviſion is to be placed. The whole are then put in motion.

MARCH!

The leader of the ſecond diviſion marches in his given direction at a ſteady pace; the commander of the regiment remains with the head diviſion, and by making it gradually advance or keep back, regulates the heads of all the others during the march, as they endeavou to continue themſelves nearly in the prolonged line of the heads
of

Halt! Wheel up! Halt, Dress! of the two leading divisions; but at any rate they are not to be before them: and when these two divisions *halt* their pivots in the line, the others, without hurrying, arrive successively in the new direction, and stand in open column at their just wheeling distances. When the head of the column is within sixty or seventy yards of the new line (its direction being already prepared) the pivot markers gallop out, and mark the pivot flanks of their several divisions.

In this manner the commander, who is himself with and conducts the two leading divisions, moves them in the direction that best answers his views, and at once takes up any position, and to any front that is necessary. As circumstances change his intentions, he may at every instant, vary and direct them upon new points of march, the other divisions of the column conforming (without the necessity of sending particular orders) to whatever alterations of direction the head may take; and the commander conducting that head so as to enable the rear to comply with its movements without hurry. During the transition, the wheeling distances should be nearly preserved by the divisions; but at any rate great care must be taken that they are correct, just before entering the new line.

S. 22. When the Regiment changes Position, by breaking into open Column of Divisions or Half Squadrons, marches to the Point in a new Line where its Head is to be placed, and enters on the Line by the Flank March of Divisions.

The pivot flank of the column being directed on the person who marks

HALT !	marks the flank point in the new line, the whole will HALT when arrived within a few yards of him ; and a point of direction 60 or 70 yards beyond is fuppofed alfo
THREE'S —— WHEEL ! MARCH ! *Halt ! Drefs !*	to be afcertained.—The divifions are then WHEELED by three's, (to the right or left as is neceffary to conduct into the new line) and the pivot markers move out to mark their points for each divifion.
MARCH !	At the word MARCH ! the whole divifions move by their flanks ; the head one places its pivot at a wheeling diftance from the perfon, and every other one in
Halt !	the manner before directed, arrange themfelves behind the head one, and behind each other ; their
Wheel up ! *Halt, Drefs !*	flanks being corrected by the commanding officer, they are then ready to *wheel* up into line.

The flank which the divifions *break* to by *three's*, and move from, will depend on which fide of the perfon they are to be arranged, and which way the line is to face.

S. 23. *When the Regiment changes Pofition by breaking into open Column of Divifions, or Half Squadrons, marching to the Point in the new Line, where its rear is to be placed, and entering on and prolonging the Line, by the fucceffive Wheels of its Divifions.*

Befides the perfon who marks the point of *entry*, two advanced points of march muft be given. The column then enters by the fucceffive wheels of its divifions

D   and

HALT! { and moves on, and when its laſt diviſion is at its point, it receives the word HALT! and pivots being corrected, the whole are ready to wheel up into line.

S. 24.   When the Regiment changes Poſition by breaking into open Column, marching to the Point in the new Line, where a central Diviſion is to be placed, and there entering on the Line.

—— *Wheel!*
Halt,   Dreſs!
March!
HALT!

{ The leading diviſion of the column having at the given point *wheeled* into the alignement, followed by the others as far as the named central diviſion ; the word HALT! is then given, and the column ſtops.

THREE'S! ——
WHEEL!
MARCH!
HALT! DRESS!

{ Such diviſions as have already wheeled into the new alignement, being now at their proper points, remain ſo.—Such diviſions as are ſtill in the old direction, are ordered to wheel by three's, to the flank which conducts to their place in the new line, and the markers move forward.

MARCH!
Halt!
Wheel up!
Halt! Dreſs!

{ At the command to MARCH! they all move on, and *halt* with their pivot flanks on it, ready to WHEEL up into line.

This movement includes both the operations of a regiment, as entering a new line, where its rear is to reſt, and where its front is to reſt.

S. 25.   When

S. 25. When the Regiment changes Posi-
tion by breaking into open Column, march-
ing to the Point in the new Line, where
its head Division is to be placed, and on
which its rear Divisions form by the Di-
agonal March of each.

Halt !

On the ———
rein back !

March !

Halt, Drefs !

March !

——— *Shoulder*
forward !
Forward !
Halt, Drefs !

The column will advance to the fpot where its leading divifion is to be placed, and will then receive the word Halt ! The leading divifion will then more accurately be placed on the new line ; and each of the other divifions will be ordered to Wheel back on its reverfe flank, as much as is necef-fary to place that flank perpendi-cular to its point in the new line. The conducting officers having placed themfelves on that flank, the whole will March and fuc-ceffively form up to the leading divifion by the diagonal move-ment. In this manner the divi-fions of the column arrive in full front, one after another, in the new line ; and that line muft face the fame way the column did.

If the column halts perpendicular to the new line, its divifions will wheel back one eighth of the circle, or a half wheel.—If the column halts oblique to the new line, the divifions will proportionally wheel fo as to be placed perpendicular to their future lines of march.

S. 26. When the open Column halts and forms in Line to the leading Divifion, and facing either to the Front or Rear, by the Divifions fucceffively paffing behind the leading one, and each other.

HALT !

> The column arrives in the direction of, or in any direction oblique or perpendicular behind the line, and HALTS.—The leading divifion either remains on its ground, or wheels to its reverfe flank, or wheels about on its reverfe flank, according to the pofition to be taken.

MARCH !
—— *Wheel!*
Halt! Drefs!
March!

—— *Wheel!*
Halt! Drefs!
March!
Halt! Drefs!

> All the pivot leaders place themfelves on the *reverfe* flank of the divifions, and eyes are turned to them.—The head divifion ftanding faft, the others are put in *motion,* and each divifion fucceffively *wheels,* and paffes clofe behind the head divifion, and again *wheels* when oppofite its place, *marches* up and *halts* to the ftanding part of the line, which is properly prolonged for the correction of their dreffing.

The divifions thus fucceffively come into line, making their wheels rapidly and fharp, fo as not to impede the following of the column.

This formation occurs when the direction of the march is nearly in the prolongation of the line, and when a regiment arriving on the flank of a line already formed has to lengthen out that line.

S, 27. When

S. 27. *When the open Column changes its Front, and leading Flank, by the Countermarch of its Divifions, each on its own Ground.*

DIVISIONS WILL COUNTERMARCH. } The column being halted, the pivot coverer takes exactly the place of his leader, but ftands with his horfe facing to the *rear.*

FROM THE ——— BY THE REAR FILE! MARCH! FORM ——DRESS! } The whole divifions then FILE from their reverfe flanks, each by its own rear, and fuch flank (now to become its pivot one) is brought up, the front rank° man to the ftationed perfon.—The following files *clofe* in to their leaders, the column ftands fquare, but facing to its former rear, and the coverer reins back to make place for the proper flank leader.—The column has thus changed its front and leading flanks.

In the countermarch, the filing is always from the flank which is not the pivot, but is to become fuch, and the conducting officers will lead out to a diftance of half the front of their divifions before they begin to countermarch.

———

This countermarch of each divifion is an evolution of great utility.—It is equivalent to the WHEEL ABOUT of each divifion of the open column, but without altering the line of pivots, or their true covering.—It at once changes the front of a column. It enables a column marching in an alignement to return along the fame line, and to take fuch new pofition in it as circumftances may require, without inverting the front of the line.— It applies to the half and quarter, as well as full and open column. In many fituations of forming from column into line, it becomes a neceffary previous operation.

- When

When a column has thus countermarched by divifions, unlefs the divifions are equal, the diftances will not be the true wheeling up ones, but will be fuch as are equal to the front of the preceding divifion, and therefore the true diftances muft be regained before the divifions can truly wheel up into line.

—————

S. 28. *When the open Column changes its leading Flank, by bringing up the rear Divifion to the Front, fucceffively followed by each other.*

	If the right of the regiment is in front, the left to be brought up, and the column to continue to advance.—The whole is ordered to
Halt!	Halt !—At the caution Left
Caution.	Wing to the front, the leader of
Three's right Wheel!	the left (the rear) divifion imme-
March!	diately orders it, *Three's right*
Halt ! Drefs !	*Wheel! March!* till his left flank
March !	can freely pafs the right flank of the others. He then commands
Halt !	*Halt ! Wheel up ! March!* clofe
Wheel up !	by the right flank of the divifion
Halt ! Drefs !	then preceding him, he himfelf
March !	being now on the right, which becomes his pivot flank.
	The officer commanding his
Three's right Wheel!	preceding divifion, as foon as the
March !	other approaches him, orders
Halt ! Drefs !	*Three's right Wheel ! March !*
March !	behind the now leading one.
Halt !	*Halt ! Wheel up !* when he co-
Wheel up !	vers, and then *March !* when
Halt ! Drefs !	at the due wheeling diftance.
March !	All the other divifions fucceffively perform the fame operation, and when

| when the right divifion has taken
| its place in the rear, the whole
| column is in perfect order, and
| proceeding in whatever direction
⎩ is given to it.

If the column before this operation ſtands clofed to
half or quarter diſtance, then each divifion proceeds as
above directed, and takes its diſtance from its preceding
one, before it moves on.

S. 29. *Change of Front, by the Counter-march of the Squadron or Regiment.*

The *countermarch* changes the front and flanks of a
body, and faces it to a rear, and is equivalent to a
wheel of the half circle, made on any of its parts or
points. It is *fucceffive*, (the body being halted) by each
of its parts wheeling fucceffively on its own ground, as
it comes to its turn. Or *progreffive*, (the body being
in motion) by each part wheeling, when it comes up
to the point at which the leading part wheeled, and begun the countermarch. In the firſt cafe, the body muſt
ſhift its ground a fpace at leaſt equal to its front.

In the fecond, it will perform this operation of the
countermarch on its original ground, exchanging flanks
and front.

The *countermarch* from one flank to the other, may
be made either before or behind the body. When from
both flanks, it will be made both before and behind the
body.—Markers will always be placed, to give the precife
ground on which the countermarch is to be made. The
column of countermarch muſt at no rate improperly
lengthen out, and the wheels of its parts muſt be firm
and rapid.

Squadron.

The squadron will countermarch from either flank—by file ; ranks by two's, or ranks by three's, in the manner prescribed for the divisions of a column.

The squadron will countermarch from one flank by sub-divisions.—Sub-divisions will wheel to the flank.—The leading one will then wheel the half circle, and proceed along the flank of the squadron, by the sub-divisions of which it is followed, till the flanks have exchanged places.

The whole being then in column, wheel to their pivots into line.

The squadron will change front to the rear, by the wheels of half squadrons.—One half squadron advances a little more than its own length, and halts.—Both half squadrons wheel about inwards.—The retired half squadron moves up and joins the other.—A half squadron or division, or any small body, may change front in the same manner, by the wheels of its half parts.

The squadron changes front by wheeling on its center. —Half the squadron goes about ranks by three's.—The squadron wheels about on its standard.—The half squadron comes about by three's, and the squadron is fronted to its former rear.—Half squadrons or divisions may change front in the same manner.

Regiment.

The regiment may countermarch from one, or from both flanks ; by the wheels of divisions, sub-divisions, ranks by three's or two's—and the squadrons of regiments will be mindful of the operation of their interval distances, by whatever kind of column they move— or it may countermarch on its center, or any other point by sub-divisions.—Or change front, each squadron by wheels of half squadron, or squadron, in the manner before directed.

S. 30. *Diminishing or increasing the Front of the Column of March.*

The column of march or manœuvre, in confequence of obftruftions in its route, which it cannot furround, is frequently obliged to diminifh its front, and again to increafe it when fuch difficulties are paffed ; it is one of the moft important of movements, and a regiment which does not perform this operation with the greateft exactnefs and attention, fo as not to lengthen out in the fmalleft degree, is not fit to move in the column of a confiderable corps.

The diminution or increafe of the front of the column, is performed by the fquadron when in movement, or when halted. In movement, this operation is either done by each divifion fucceffively, when it arrives at the point where the leading one of the column performed it ; or elfe by the whole divifions of the fquadron at the fame moment. In either cafe, the chief of the fquadron, at the inftant that it fhould begin to reduce or increafe its front, gives the general CAUTION fo to do, and the leaders of divifions give their words of execution to the fub-divifions to double behind, or move up brifkly to the regulating ones, which preferve their original diftances from each other, and never alter the pace at which the column was marching, but proceed as if they were totally unconnected with the operation that the others are performing.

CLOSE COLUMN.

The great object of a confiderable clofe column is, to form the line to the front in the quickeft manner poffible ; to conceal numbers from the knowledge of the adverfary ; and to extend in whatever direction the circumftance of the cafe may require, which, till it is nearly accomplifhed, cannot be obvious to an oppofite enemy. It is a fituation for the affembly, more than for the movement of troops. It is not formed until the head of
the

the troops is arrived in column, of whole, half, or quarter diftance, near the ground where they are to extend into line.

The formation from clofe column into line, is an original one; often protected by cannon, made at fuch a diftance, as not to fear interruption from an enemy; and avoiding the enfilade of artillery. Its pofitions cannot fail to be truly taken.

The clofe column may generally be compofed of half fquadrons, for the purpofe of movement. But when halted and to deploy, it may then double its front, and ftand in fquadrons.

In the clofe column, when ready to deploy into line, there is a diftance of two horfes' length between regiment and regiment—of one horfe's length between fquadrons of the regiment—of half a horfe's length between the divifions and ranks of fquadrons. Officers and their coverers, are on the pivot flanks of their divifions— colours and fupernumeraries are on the flanks, not the pivot ones; and mufic, farriers, or certain fupernumeraries, may alfo be in the rear of the regiment, no fingle perfons are between the ranks.

When the clofe column is formed and halted, the commanding officer (alone) gives orders for its MARCH! HALT! and commencement of formation in line.

A clofe column muft loofen its divifions before it can well march in front, and its changes of direction muft be made circling, and on a moving flank, to enable its rear gradually to comply. If too great intervals fhould be made in the column, they can beft be clofed by a halt of the head.

The clofe column is formed from line, or from the column of march.

When the regiment from line forms clofe column, it is neceffary to difengage the heads of its divifions from one another, that they may the fooner and eafier arrive at their pofition; this they do, *by wheeling to the hand ordered an eighth wheel* (of the quarter circle), they then
wheel

wheel ranks by threes to their leading flank, march to their place in column, and each wheels up by threes, which again forms the divifion.

———

S. 31. *The clofe Column may be formed from Line in front or rear of either of the Flank Half Squadrons, or in front or rear of any central one.*

If the Column is to ftand faced as the Line is.

1. If in front of a flank divifion—the eighth wheel is outwards, or from that divifion, and three's break to their front leading flank.

2. If in rear of a flank divifion, the eighth wheel is inwards, or towards that divifion ; and the three's break to their rear or leading hand.

3. If in front and rear of a central divifion—the eighth wheel is towards the hand which is to be the head of the column ; viz. to the right, if the right is to be in front ; and to the left, if the left is to be in front ; and the three's break to their conducting hand.

———

If the Column is to ftand faced to the Rear.

1. If in front of a flank divifion—that divifion is countermarched, the eighth wheel is made outwards, or from that divifion; and three's break to what was the ftanding flank, or their rear hand.

2. If in rear of a flank divifion—that divifion is countermarched, the eighth wheel is inwards, or to that divifion ; and three's break to the flank that wheeled up, or their front hand.

3. If in front and rear of a central divifion—that divifion is countermarched, the eighth wheel is towards
the

the flank, which is to be the head of the column—and the divisions break by three's to their conducting hand.

On this occasion advantage will arise, if the *eighth wheel* is made on the center of each body, which does so wheel; as it will more effectually disengage the leading flanks.

S. 32. *When the Regiment from Line forms close Column.*

1. *Before or behind either of the Flank Half Squadrons.*

CAUTION.	A CAUTION will express the half squadron, and whether the formation is in front or rear of it : and a new position may be given to it, and its leader shifts, if necessary, to that flank which is to become the pivot one of the column, and another person places himself ten or twenty yards before or behind him, according to circumstances, to mark the perpendicular and pivot line of the column.
HALF SQUADRONS TO THE—WHEEL! MARCH! HALT! DRESS!	The half squadrons of the regiment will eight wheel (of the quarter circle) to the hand ordered.
THREE's--WHEEL! MARCH! *Halt, Dress!*	The half squadrons will WHEEL by three's, to which ever hand conducts them to their place in the close column, and leaders will shift accordingly.
MARCH!	The whole will MARCH to the front or rear of the named half squadron,

Halt !
Wheel up !
Halt ! Drefs !

fquadron, and each leader will proceed in the fame manner as in forming open column from line (except that pivot markers are not fent out) ftopping in his own perfon at his pivot point, and giving his words to *halt, wheel up,* and *drefs,* to his half fquadron, when it has arrived upon the proper ground on which it is to ftand in clofe column.

During the formation of the clofe column, as foon as the regiment is put in motion, the commanding officer will immediately place himfelf before the officer of the directing half fquadron, and fee that the pivot leaders cover each other in the perpendicular direction, whether fuch covering is taken from before or behind.

2. *On a central Half Squadron.*

CAUTION.

A CAUTION of formation is given. ——The named half fquadron will ftand faft, or be otherwife placed ; its leader will place himfelf on its future pivot flank, and the line of pivots will be afcertained by a detached perfon.

—— EIGHTH
WHEEL !
MARCH !
Halt ! Drefs !
THREE'S ——
WHEEL !
MARCH !
HALT ! DRESS !

The half fquadrons of the regiment will wheel towards the hand which is to be in front of the column, and leaders will fhift accordingly.

MARCH !

MARCH! *Halt!* *Wheel up!* *Halt! Drefs!*	At the word MARCH! the reft of the formation will proceed as before directed, part of the regiment arranging itfelf before and part behind the given half fquadron, and the officers covering on the proper pivot flank.

In forming clofe column facing to the rear, the fame operations take place as to the front, with this difference, that the named half fquadron countermarches; and the other half fquadrons of the regiment wheel as directed, and lead from fuch flanks as eftablifh a countermarch of the whole.

In the fame manner in which clofe columns are here formed from line, may *columns at half or quarter diftance* alfo generally be formed, obferving that in fuch cafes, pivot flank points are given by markers, as in the formation in open column.

If the clofe column of fquadrons is formed from line.— The intervals between them prevent the neceffity of their making the eight wheel:—they will, therefore, at once break by three's to their leading flank, and march to their places in column, as before directed.

S. 33. *When the Column marches to a Flank.*

CAUTION.	A CAUTION will exprefs to which flank. If to that which is not the pivot, the leading officer and coverer of each is ORDERED to move quickly by the rear of their divifions to that flank, and the ferrefiles and colours who were

	were on that flank, exchange to the other.
THREE'S TO THE —WHEEL ! MARCH ! Halt ! Drefs ! MARCH !	The whole will WHEEL by three's to the flank, and be put in MARCH, the officer that leads the front divifion taking care to move in the exact alignement which is prolonged for him, and all the others, in preferving their proper fituations, drefs and move by him.
HALT ! WHEEL UP ! HALT ! DRESS !	When the the column HALTS and WHEELS UP by three's, the pivot leaders are ORDERED to fhift to their proper places (if not already at them) by the rear of their divifions, unlefs the intended and immediate formation of the line, requires their remaining where they are.

S. 34. *When the Column marches to the Front.*

| MARCH ! CAUTION ! HALT ! March ! HALT ! | The whole advance at the word MARCH ! If it is intended to loofen the column, a CAUTION fo to do will be given, the whole will HALT, except the leading divifion, and each divifion will again fucceffively *march* at a horfe's diftance. |
| | When the general word HALT ! is given, the column halts as it is then placed ; but if a partial and low word *Halt !* is given to the leading divifion only, the others move on ftill, and *halt* fucceffively |

in

in clofe column, by word from
their leaders.

S. 35. *When the Column is to change Direction.*

If halted.

CAUTION !

A CAUTION will be given that
it is to change direction either to
the right or left. The front divifion of the column is *wheeled* up
into the new direction, and an
advanced perfon is placed to determine the future line of pivots.

THREE'S WHEEL !
MARCH !
Halt ! Drefs !
MARCH !
Halt !
Wheel up !
Halt ! Drefs !

The other divifions will WHEEL
by three's to the ordered flank ;
MARCH ! *Halt ! Wheel up !* and
cover in column. If this movement is made by the reverfe flank,
no fhifting of leaders will be required, but one of the ferrefile
officers already there, will conduct the flank movement of each,
the words of command being ftill
given by the proper pivot leader
to *halt* and *wheel up.*

If in march.

If gradual and inconfiderable changes of direction are
to be made during the march of the columns, the HEAD
will, on a moveable pivot, effect fuch change, while all
the other divifions, by advancing a fhoulder, and inclining up to the flank which is the wheeling one, will
fucceffively conform to each other, and to the leading
divifion,

divifion, fo that at the word *forward*, they may move on in the ftraight line.

S. 36. *When the Column is to make Front to its Rear, by the Countermarch of its Divifions.*

THE COLUMN WILL COUNTER-MARCH!
> If the divifions are at a fufficient distance to allow of it, they will each feparately, on its own ground, countermarch, as directed for open column.

EVEN DIVISIONS, RIGHT FILE! MARCH! *Form!*
> If the column is quite clofe, the whole will prepare to *file* from the reverfe flank. The even, or every other divifion (reckoning from the head) will *file* to the flank, and form, fo that their pivot flank may be three or four paces clear of the column.

THE WHOLE WILL COUNTERMARCH! MARCH! *Halt! Form! Drefs!*
> They are then ordered to COUNTERMARCH towards the column, and at the fame word, the odd divifions, which have hitherto ftood ftill, countermarch alfo, each on its own ground; the even divifions *file* on till they are again in their proper places in column, and *halt, form*.

DEPLOYMENT INTO LINE.

The clofe column of the regiment forms in line on its front, or its rear, or on any central divifion, by the DEPLOYMENT or flank march by three's, and by which it fucceffively uncovers and extends its feveral divifions.

E   *Before*

Before the clofe column deploys, its head divifion, whether it is halted or in movement, muft be on the line into which it is to extend. That line is therefore the prolongation of the head divifion, and fuch points in it, to one or both flanks, as are neceffary for the formation of the regiment, are immediately taken.

The flank march muft be made quick, parallel to the general line, and without opening out, the moft particular precifion is therefore required. Each divifion, when oppofite to its ground in line, will be moft advantageoufly halted, and wheeled up (or at leaft corrected) by a detached field officer of the regiment; in cafe its leader fhould not be critical in his commands, or, that he fhould not be heard; or, that his three's are too open; and thus may the defects of a preceding divifion be remedied, by the judicious ftop of the one following it. The divifion is then brought up into line by its refpective leader. The juftnefs of formations depends altogether on officers judging their diftances, and timing their commands.

The officer, in leading his divifion into line, muft bring it up perfectly fquare. His dreffing is always from the laft come up divifion, towards the other flank, and the eyes of all are turned to that divifion, and the formed part of the line.

As the head of the clofe column is always brought up to the line on which it is to extend, therefore, when the formation is made on the rear, or on a central divifion, fuch divifion, when uncovered, muft move up to the identical ground which the front has quitted.

S. 37. *When the Regiment in clofe Column of Half Squadrons,* (fuppofe the Right in Front) *deploys into Line.*

1. *On the front Divifion.*

The column being halted with its front divifion in the alignement

Caution.

ment, and all the others in their true fituations, parallel, and well clofed up to it, a point of forming and dreffing upon is taken, in the prolongation of that divifion (before the flanks of which two markers are placed) and towards where the left of the regiment is to extend. A caution is given that the line will form on the front divifion.

Three's left Wheel! March! Halt! Dreſs!

At the words, Three's left wheel! March! Halt! Dreſs! the front divifion ftands faft, its leader fhifting to the right, and all the others wheel, (in this cafe always to the pivot flank).

March!

At the word March! they go off quick, with heads dreffed, moving parallel (not oblique) to the line of formation, the three's clofe and compact, fo as not to open the divifions out.

Halt! Wheel up! Halt! Dreſs! March!

The leader of the fecond or leading divifion having moved out to his right, at the above word, march, allows his divifion, led by his coverer, to go on a fpace equal to its front (ferrefiles exclufive) and then gives his words, Halt! Wheel up! Halt, Dreſs! and corrects and fquares his divifion, then brings it to the alignement, giving the words, March! Halt, Dreſs! leaving the accurate dreffing to the fquadron officer, who is on the right flank (of fquadron) for that purpofe.

Halt! Dreſs!

In this manner every other divifion proceeds, each being fuc-

E 2   ceffively

{ ceffively fronted, marched up, and
{ halted.

The divifions, which give the intervals of fquadrons, muft take care to front oppofite their ground in line, and fend up a marker to give the interval flank. The ftandard will come up in its place with the right half fquadron. The ferrefiles will halt when their divifions front; and when the movement of the other divifions allow of it, they will place themfelves behind their own proper ones.

---

2. *On the Rear Divifion.*

The column being placed as before directed, and a point of forming taken to the right in the prolongation of the head divifion, and towards where the right of the regiment is to come.

CAUTION. { A CAUTION is given, that the line will be formed on the rear divifion. The leaders of divifions, and their coverers (except thofe of the rear divifion) will immediately be ORDERED to pafs behind their feveral divifions, and poft themfelves on the right of each, exchanging places with their ferrefiles.

Two under officers are fent from the rear divifion, to place themfelves exactly before the flank files of the front divifion, and the leader of the front divifion is fhewn the point in the alignement on which he is to march, taking his intermediate points if neceffary.

The

THREE'S RIGHT WHEEL! MARCH! Halt! Drefs!	The words, THREE'S RIGHT WHEEL! MARCH! Halt, Drefs! are then given, and all the divifions, except the rear one, wheel threes to the right (in this cafe always to the reverfe flank.)
MARCH!	At the word MARCH! the wheeled divifions move on quick; their heads are dreffed to the left; the front one moves in the alignement, and the others parallel, and clofe on its right.
March!	As foon as the rear divifion is uncovered, it receives the word, March! and proceeds. When within a few yards of its ground, its leader moves brifkly up to the marker of its left in the new pofition, and there in due time gives
Halt! Drefs!	his words, Halt, Drefs! quickly correcting his divifion on the diftant point of formation.
Halt! Wheel up! Halt! Drefs!	In the mean time the leader of the divifion which immediately precedes the rear one, having at the firft word MARCH! gone brifkly round to the rear of his divifion, without impeding its movement, and having allowed it to move on, led by his coverer, gives his words to Halt! Wheel up! Halt, Drefs! when his divifion has marched a diftance equal to its front, and thereby uncovered the one behind it (which as already mentioned, immediately moves forward) he then places himfelf on its left. As foon as his own front is clear, he
March!	gives his word, March! his divifion proceeds to the alignement,

where

Halt, Drefs!

where he gives his words *Halt, Drefs!* when his own left joins the right of the half fquadron formed on. The fquadron officers dreffing and correcting as in the preceding deployment. The markers of intervals, ftandard, and ferrefiles, proceed as already mentioned.

All the other divifions fucceffively are conducted in the fame manner, until the right one (which has been marching critically in the alignement, and on no account getting before it) receives, when it arrives on its juft ground, the words to *Halt! Wheel up!* and *Drefs!*

Halt! Wheel up!
Halt, Drefs!

3. *On a Central Divifion.*

Forming points muft be given to both flanks in the prolongation of the head divifion. At the CAUTION of forming on a central divifion, the leading officers, and ferrefiles, will fhift accordingly. The divifions in front of the named one wheel to one flank; thofe in the rear of it to the other; according to the hand which leads to their ground. The named divifion, when uncovered, moves up into line to its marked flank; thofe that were in front of it proceed as in forming on a rear divifion; thofe that are in the rear of it, proceed as in forming on a front divifion.

S. 38. *Oblique Deployment of the clofe Column into Line.*

1. *On an oblique Line advanced.*

The front divifion is wheeled up into a new direction on its *reverfe* flank, and the line is prolonged.
The

The divifions of the column are wheeled up to the hand it deploys to. The leaders of divifions then turn their horfes fo as themfelves to take a direction parallel to the given one. The whole are put in march, and the rear of the divifions gradually get into the fquare direction of their heads, which proceed and form as ufual.

In this movement the heads of the divifions will be a little retired behind each other, the rear leaders will take great care not to clofe on each other, nor the head which conducts them. Much precifion is alfo required in juftly timing the *Halt, Wheel up!* of each divifion, which by that time ought to be moving perfectly parallel to the line of formation.

2. *On an oblique Line retired.*

The front divifion is wheeled upon its pivot flank into the new direction, and the line is prolonged. The fame operation, though more difficult, takes place, as when the line is advanced, and the rear divifions muft take particular care to eafe from and yield to the march of the front. The head divifion being advanced a few paces before it takes the oblique direction, will give a facility to the heads of the rear divifions in gradually gaining it.

Such deployment can hardly be required on any other than the front divifion of the clofe column. Particular attention is neceffary, to give every aid as to the points of forming, and to the heads of divifions moving as foon as poffible parallel to and behind the line.

S. 39. *When the clofe Column halted is to form in Line in the Prolongation of its Flanks, and on a front, or rear, or central Divifion.*

{ The caution of formation is
{ given. The named divifion ftands

F 4   faft.

MARCH!

Halt!

THREE'S ABOUT!
MARCH!
HALT, DRESS!
MARCH!
Halt! Front!
Halt! Drefs!

faſt, the others march forward
in cloſe column in the given line.
Their pivot officers ſucceſſively
take wheeling diſtance from each
other, beginning at the named one,
and ſucceſſively give their word
halt! as each has acquired it.
When the whole is in open column, the line is formed by a
wheel up to a flank. In this
manner diſtances are begun to be
taken from the rear. But when
the named diviſion is a front or
central one, the others that are
behind it muſt wheel three's
about, MARCH forward, take
their diſtances, and FRONT ſucceſſively.

The column may alſo be opened from any named
diviſion, by the leading one only marching off and each
other ſucceſſively following, as wheeling diſtance is acquired from the one preceding. When the whole have
opened, the general word HALT! is given, or the column is allowed to proceed.

---

*S. 40. When the Column cloſed to half
diſtance forms in Line to its Front on any
Diviſion.*

The line will be formed either by the deployments of
the cloſe column, or by the flank marches of the diviſions of the open column, and there wheel up into line;
or by a ſharp incline of diviſions into line. In every
caſe, care muſt be taken to have a ſufficiency of points
eſtabliſhed to enſure the true direction of the line.

From column at quarter diſtance the line may be
formed to any front, and on any diviſion, by the movements of the cloſe and open column.

CHANGES

CHANGES OF POSITION OF THE REGIMENT BY THE ECHELLON (or diagonal) MOVEMENT.

The echellon pofition and movements are not only ne-ceffary and applicable to the immediate attacks and retreats of great bodies, but alfo to the previous *oblique* or direct changes of fituation, which a regiment or corps formed in line, may be obliged to make to its front or rear, or on a particular fixed divifion of the line.

Echellon of march in changes of pofition.

The oblique changes are produced by the wheel lefs than the quarter circle, of divifions from line, which places them in the echellon fituation, ready to move. The *direct* changes are produced by the perpendicular and fucceffive march of divifions from line, to front or rear.

How form-ed.

The march in the direct echellon produces new parallel pofitions to front or rear. The march in echellon when formed by the wheels of the divifions from line, pro-duces new oblique pofitions to front or rear, and at the fame time to the flank, according to the degree of wheel given to the echellon.

How ap-plied.

The march in open column produces new prolonged pofitions to either flank.

The echellon of march neceffary in making changes of fituation, will be compofed of half-fquadrons or divi-fions, and formed from line by the wheel of each for-ward on its own flank, to the hand to which it is to move, and fuch wheel muft be lefs than the quarter circle, for in fuch cafe the body would be in open column.

To form the echellon of oblique march, the degree of wheel made up from line ought ftrictly to be fuch as will place the divifions perpendicular to their future points of march; but in practice generally, the *half*, *quarter*, or *eighth wheel* (of the quarter circle) each or-dered according to circumftances, may fuffice to attain the proper end.

Degree of wheel into echellon.

The echellon may be confidered as a column of a par-ticular kind, as well as the open column ; they are eafily
converted

converted into each other, by a new degree of wheel of each of their component divifions.

S. 41. *When from Line, the Half-fquadrons of a Regiment march off in Echellon fucceffively and directly forward to the Front and again form in Line, either to the Front or to the Flank.*

1. *As long as the intention is to form again to that front*—They may be retired at any *named* diftance behind each other, and when the leading divifion *halts*, the others may move on, and drefs in line with it.

2. *But when the intention is to form in line to the flank* —The whole will be ordered to HALT, or the divifions to take any named diftance and *halt*. The directing flank of the leading divifion will be confidered as the firft point in the intended oblique line, and the particular direction meant to be given it, will be eftablifhed by the placing of another point beyond and before it. A marker from each divifion will quickly move out, and place themfelves as pivots, lining on the firft given points, and on each other ; each alfo taking a diftance from the one before him, equal to the front of the divifion which precedes him.

The rear divifions are then, by inclining to their directing hands, or by flank marching, moving up, and fhoulders forward, MARCHED to their refpective markers, and halted on the line. Or the divifions, inftead of forming in line, may be ordered to HALT in echellon at their feveral markers, and parallel to their former front. The whole is then put in march forward, and preferving their relative fituations, HALT, and WHEEL BACK into line, at fome more advanced point.

S. 42. *When a Regiment from Line wheels forward by Half Squadrons or Divisions to either Flank, into oblique Echellon, and Halts.*

CAUTION.

DIVISIONS WILL MAKE AN EIGHT WHEEL TO—— !

> At the general CAUTION—That the divisions will wheel forward, so as to place them perpendicular to their future lines of march; a person from the leading division of each squadron marks the wheeling flank of that division, according to the degree ordered, whether *half*, *quarter*, or *eighth wheel.*

MARCH!
HALT! DRESS!

> At the word MARCH! each division wheels up, and they receive the words HALT, DRESS! to the standing flank, to which the leaders of divisions (as necessary) have shifted.

When the movement is to be the rear instead of the front—the regiment will wheel about by three's; wheel forward into echellon, in the above manner; and proceed as if the line was to its proper front.

S. 43. *When a Regiment or Line is to change its Position on a fixed Flank, by throwing the other Flank forward or backward, and by the Echellon march of Divisions.*

1. *When a Flank is thrown forward.*

The new direction is ascertained by two persons, placed beyond the flank, and the flank division is accurately wheeled into it.

DIVISIONS

| DIVISIONS— WHEEL! MARCH! HALT! DRESS! | The other fimilar divifions of the line are (each upon its inward flank) wheeled up *half* as much as the flank divifion wheeled, and thus ftand in echellon, the pivot leaders placing themfelves on the inward flank. |
| MARCH! | The whole, except the flank divifion, are then put in MARCH, each looking to its leader, who is on its inward flank, and thus advancing perpendicularly towards its point in the new line. |

Before the leading divifion of each fquadron has reached the line, a marker will move forward quickly to prolong it, and place himfelf rather beyond where his rear divifion is to come up; fo that there fhall be always at leaft one fixed object to correct upon beyond each divifion, as it halts in line.

| *Shoulders forward!* *Forward!* *Halt, Drefs!* | When the officer, conducting the fecond divifion, arrives within twenty or twenty-five paces of where he is to join the firft divifion already placed, he gives a word, *Shoulder* (the outward one) *forward!* on which the man next to himfelf gradually turns his horfe, fo as to arrive in the new line, perfectly fquare in his own perfon; and the reft of his divifion (who till this inftant have marched in their original perpendicular direction) conforming to him, and proportionally quickening their pace, arrive in full parallel front on the line, fo as to have a very fmall movement to make at the words *Halt! Drefs!* which is given when his leading flank touches the flank of his preceding divifion; and inftantly refumes |

fumes

fumes his place in fquadron, leaving the correct dreffing to the
fquadron officer.

Shoulders forward!
Forward!
Halt! Drefs!

In this manner divifion will
come up after divifion, each following one obferving to give the
word *Shoulders forward!* when
the preceding one gets the words
Halt! Drefs! and each, after
bringing up his divifion, fhifts to
his poft in fquadron.

The exact formation in this oblique line depends totally on the divifions having wheeled (only) one half of
the angle, which the new pofition makes with the old
one; for fhould they at firft wheel up the whole of
that angle, they would then be marching parallel to
that line, and arrive in it doubled behind each other;
whereas, by having the other half of the wheel to complete when they come near to the new pofition, each
moves in a perpendicular direction, and difengages the
ground required by the fucceeding one to form upon.

------

2. *When a Flank is thrown backward.*

The direction is afcertained as before, and the flank
divifion *placed* on it.

THREE'S ABOUT!
MARCH!
HALT! DRESS!

The fquadrons of the line go
about ranks by three's.

DIVISIONS—
WHEEL!
MARCH!
HALT! DRESS!

The divifions of fquadrons
make their *ordered degree* of
wheel towards the placed divifion.

MARCH!

The divifions MARCH with the
rear ranks in front, and form in
line, in the fame manner as when
changing pofition forward; except

<table>
<tr><td>

—Shoulder
forward !
Forward !

</td><td>

cept that the leader of each, when he arrives within twenty or twenty-five paces of the line, will give his word, *Shoulder forward !* and thereby gradually bring up his division to be parallel to the line; he himself having ftopt at the line, will, as foon as his flank front rank man comes to the preceding formed rear rank man, give his words to

</td></tr>
<tr><td>

Halt, front !
Halt ! Drefs !
March !
Halt ! Drefs !

</td><td>

Halt ! Front ! Halt ! Drefs ! March ! Halt ! Drefs ! in the general line on the point which is prepared for him beyond the flank of his own fquadron.

</td></tr>
</table>

Very great activity is required from the leader in dreffing up, or dreffing back of his divifion, otherwife the point of appui (viz. his own fartheft flank) will not be ready for the next leader, who is to arrive at and begin from it to perform the fame operation, and this will particularly happen where the change of direction is inconfiderable.

In the fucceffive dreffing up or back of divifions, officers are to be careful always to line them, fo as not to obfcure the marking perfons, but to leave them open and diftinct, fo that the direction of the line may run horfe's head to horfe's head of the markers.

────────

3. *When the Change is on a Central Divifion, one Flank being thrown forward, and the other backward.*

The direction of the new line is afcertained, and the central divifion placed on it.

<table>
<tr><td>

THREE'S ABOUT !
March !
Halt ! Drefs !

</td><td>

The fquadrons of the retiring wing go ABOUT by three's.

</td></tr>
</table>

DIVI-

| DIVISIONS- RIGHT WHEEL ! MARCH ! HALT, DRESS ! | The divifions of the fquadrons of each wing make the *ordered* , *degree* of wheel inwards and forwards, fo as to face to the placed divifion. |
| MARCH ! | The whole MARCH forward into line with the central divifion, the advancing wing dreffing up, and the retiring wing again fronting and dreffing in line; as already defcribed. |

S. 44. *March in Line.*

The march of the line in front is the moft difficult, and the moft material of all movements; it is requifite near the enemy, and immediately precedes the attack. In proportion to the extent of front, and rapidity required, does that difficulty encreafe; therefore too much exactnefs and minutenefs in the execution of it cannot be obferved.

March in line.

When marching in line, each fquadron dreffes to its own center, which center follows its own leader, the feveral leaders line with, and preferve diftances from each other, and from the regulating fquadron; this alone has its objects of march, the others being all fubordinate to, and conforming to its motions.

General Attention.

When parts of a line marching in front are interrupted by any obftacle, they muft halt, and by flank movements of their divifions or fubdivifions, double behind (into clofe column) fuch adjoining parts as are not fo interrupted, and avoid preffing upon them. In proportion as they pafs fuch obftacle, and that the ground permits them to come into line, they will in the fame manner, by flank movements, move up into their proper places, where a void fpace has been preferved for them. If only fmall portions of a line are interrupted, and for a fhort fpace, they may follow in file, or rather in ranks,

Paffing obftacles.

Column.

by

by three's or two's behind the flanks of the uninterrupted parts, and move up to their places in file (or by three's or two's) when it can be done.

Halt of the line.

When the line halts, each fquadron halts and dreffes by its own center; and if the dreffing of the general line is to be afterwards corrected, it ought to begin at, and be taken from the regulating fquadron.

Succeffive halt of fquadrons.

The line fhould always be in fo correct a fituation, as to halt inftantly at the word, *Halt !* but if at any time the difficulties of ground have unavoidably thrown fquadrons out of the line, in fuch cafe, the halt of thofe fquadrons will be fucceffive as they regain their proper fituations.

Standards.

The ftandards muft be always carried uniformly and upright, in order to facilitate the moving and dreffing of the line.

Dreffing the line after halting.

After the march and halt in line of each fquadron by its own center, if a more exact dreffing is required, then two perfons are placed with their horfes heads before the flank files of the regulating fquadron, which is previoufly dreft in the true direction ; each other fquadron, from each flank, advances (directly forward) a perfon to prolong that line ; all eyes are directed to the regulating fquadron ; the whole (by fquadrons, either together or fucceffively, and quickly as ordered), move up and halt in the given line. A ftraight line is in this manner obtained ; but if the intervals are falfe, they muft remain fo till corrected, by order, and by a feparate operation of flank marching.

Flank fquadron.

A flank-fquadron of a line need never remain an inftant with a faife interval, or ill dreffed, as its corrections do not interfere with any part of the line.

S. 45. When the Line advances.

A line that is to advance, muft be before hand accurately formed and dreffed, to enable it to move in a direction perpendicular to its front, otherwife a floating, open-

opening out, or clofing in of its parts, will take place, till fuch perpendicular march is attained.

THE LINE WILL ADVANCE !

{ THE LINE WILL ADVANCE (by a named fquadron), is a caution. The officer commanding fuch fquadron, quickly determines by his eye the exact perpendicular to the front of the line which he is to march upon, and till he is fatisfied the direction of it is juft, he is not to look out for objects in it. Every other fquadron remains prepared.

Any perfon, who means to indicate the direction of a line which is to be purfued (and the prolongation of which is not upon fome ftrong object) to another perfon, will do it in the moft ready manner, by himfelf riding fome fmall diftance forward in the intended direction, and defiring the perfon who has remained at a given point to take fuch line over his head, and of courfe to mark his points of marching in it.

MARCH !

{ At the word MARCH ! inftantly repeated to each fquadron, the whole move ; each fquadron by its center, and each fquadron leader attentive to, and preferving his pace, line, and diftance, from his directing hand. If the whole move uniformly and ftraight forward, the line will be firm and fteady. If any inaccuracy arifes, it muft be inftantly remedied by the inclining, moving up, or keeping back of particular fquadrons, and fuch neceffary alterations muft be made, by firm command and judicious execution, fo as not to affect the general line. The attention of commanding officers is extended to the general line, and they are to avoid partaking of errors of any

F   portion

portion of it, that is evidently in the wrong; but, on the contrary, to confider fuch part as if deranged by fome occafional obftacle, and to preferve their own juft relative pofition with refpect to the directing fquadron.

HALT!

If the line marches juft, it will halt juftly, the whole at the fame inftant of the command HALT! If this is not the cafe, the halt of fquadrons muft be to a degree fucceffive; at any rate the fquadrons muft halt in the general line.

All alterations of pace muft be made in a firm and decided manner, and by the whole at the fame inftant, in confequence of the order repeated by fquadron leaders.

S. 46. *When the Line retires.*

THE neceffity of its being previoufly and correctly dreffed, is full as effential as when it is to advance; if that preliminary is not taken care of, its movements will be difordered in proportion to its extent.

THE LINE WILL RETIRE!

THE LINE WILL RETIRE, is a Caution—on which preparation is made in the fame manner as on advancing; the officer who leads the directing fquadron, immediately afcertains his point of march, and each fquadron has an officer (not the commanding one) placed behind its center, ready to lead to the rear.

THREE'S ABOUT!
MARCH!
HALT! DRESS!

RANKS BY THREE'S ABOUT—MARCH! on which the ranks and ferrefiles wheel about, and the fquadrons remain ready for the general word.

MARCH!

MARCH !	MARCH !—The line retires in the fame manner as it advances, and the commanding officers of fquadrons, being in the rear of the ftandards (each of his own) can by their eye and directions, give occafional aid.
HALT !	HALT—is the paufe of a moment.
FRONT !	RANKS—by three's about.
HALT ! DRESS !	HALT ! DRESS ! by the ftandards.

If any further dreffing of the line is neceffary, it is ordered by the commander as already directed.

The line is never to remain halted an inftant after facing to the rear, but is immediately to march on. And when it halts, it is immediately to FRONT, and then to DRESS.

When the line is marching to the front or rear, the partial obftacles that prefent themfelves, will be paffed by the formation, march, and deployment of the clofe column. Such parts as are not interrupted ftill move on in front ; fuch parts as are interrupted double by divifions as ordered behind an adjoining flank, or flanks, and in this manner follow in clofe column in their natural order. As the ground opens they fucceffively deploy, and again perfect the line. The columns are always behind the line, and march clofed up. The formed part of the regiments, whether advancing or retiring, continues to move on at the ordinary pace, and in proportion as the obftacles increafe or diminifh, will the formed, or column, parts of the line increafe or diminifh.

S. 47. *Retreat of the Regiment by alternate Half Squadrons.*

The regiment is told off by alternate, right and left, half fquadrons, and one of direction for each is announced.

One

One divifion of the regiment (the left) is ordered to ftand faft, the rights go three's about.

The retiring part marches a given diftance, and when ordered, halts and fronts; this ferves for a fignal to the advanced part of the regiment to begin its retreat in the fame manner, each body through its proper interval; and, when ordered, to halt and front. The alternate retreat is thus continued either at a walk or at a trot, till the line has attained fome new fituation, being covered by fuch fkirmifhers or light troops, as were originally advanced in the front for that purpofe, and who gradually fall back in proportion as the lines do.

Inverfion of the Line.

The fquadrons may be obliged to wheel by ranks or divifions to the right about, the more readily to oppofe a danger, inftead of changing a pofition by a counter-march. It may be under the neceffity of forming to a flank, its rear rank in front. The column with its right in front may arrive on the left of its ground, and be obliged immediately to form up, and fupport that point. But on the whole, it is to be recollected, that though the inverfion of fquadrons in a regiment ought to occafion no real inconvenience, yet that of the divifions of the fquadron within itfelf, would lead to diforder, and muft be ftudioufly avoided.

S. 48. *When without the help of advanced Objects, the Commander of a Line changes the pofition of the whole, or Part of it, to a Flank.*

In original formations of the line from column of march, preparatory points can always be given; *but, in changes of the line, or parts of it,* from one pofition to another, more advantageous with refpect to the enemy, and to making the attack, the new one muft often depend

pend on, and be taken up by, the eye of the commander only, while the whole is in motion, and who will himfelf conduct the movement.

The change being determined on, the movement being neceffarily a quick one, and the body that is to make it being apprized accordingly, the commander places himfelf at the flank which is to lead, and has five or fix detached perfons with him, ready to take his orders.

The line breaks into column to the flank, (of divifions, fub-divifions, or ranks by three's, according as the ground allows; for in fuch an operation the column muft be on fuch a front as it can maintain, till it again forms in line); on this occafion, the pivots being lined, and the wheeling diftances being true, is moft effential, and therefore if the divifions can form column backwards, it fhould be done.

The commander being before the pivot of the leading divifion puts the whole in motion, and conducts the head of the column, in fuch manner as he finds proper, towards the ground on which he propofes to form a new line, and to the pace and path of which head, the reft of the column muft ftrictly conform.

When he arrives near to where he propofes his formation, with a glance of the eye, without ftopping, and according to the enemy's fituation, he determines the direction he is to give his line, and the point where he means to enter it, conducting his leading divifion, fo as by a circling movement of the *fhoulder forward,* to arrive with its pivot flank on the line on that point, he there halts a perfon to indicate the point of entry, (with his horfe's head to the flank of the column) and purfues the direction, which is only known to himfelf, and in which he will always find and take intermediate points. From diftance to diftance he leaves perfons placed in the above manner in the line, for the direction of the column points, which they are to take care fucceffively to pafs clofe to. He HALTS the column when he finds neceffary. *Wheels* up into line—Is ready TO ADVANCE—And, ATTACK, in line or echellon.

F 3   S. 49.

S. 49.   *Paſſage of Lines.*

If ſquadrons are to paſs through infantry in their front.   When the line arrives cloſe behind them, each ſquadron will march from its center ranks by two's (eight men in front).   They will all paſs at the ſame inſtant through the openings which are made for them, and at the diſtance of thirty yards the heads will halt and dreſs, the ſquadrons will form, and the line move on.

If the line has attacked and broken the enemy, and that ſmaller detachments than ſquadrons are to purſue, they will at the ordered inſtant march from a flank, ranks by two's, paſs the infantry, form up while in motion, and purſue with vigour.

A line of cavalry obliged to retire through a line of infantry, will, when arrived cloſe to the infantry, front, and inſtantly march off each half ſquadron (from its right flank) ranks by two's, ſtraight to the rear, wherever the heads of half-ſquadrons preſent themſelves, the infantry will make opening ſufficient for four horſes to paſs through.   The heads of the half-ſquadrons remain dreſſed, and preſerve diſtances from the left.   When at a ſufficient diſtance (in the rear) the open column is formed (right in front) by the cloſing in and wheeling up of the two's.   Pivots being then adjuſted, the parallel line is formed by the wheeling up of the half-ſquadrons.

S. 50.   *Attack of Cavalry in Front and Flank.*

The covering a flank in a line of cavalry, or having a body behind a flank, ready to turn that of the enemy, is of the greateſt conſequence, and their previous ſituation ſhould be concealed as much as poſſible.   That flank which is not to be employed in turning the enemy, cannot be ſo well ſecured as by two or three half-ſquadrons

drons placed in echellon to the firft line, about fifty paces from each other. With difficulty the enemy can turn this echellon, and it enables the other flank to act with more freedom. Thefe half-fquadrons in echellon are kept refufed or brought up into line according to circumftances.

But behind the flank deftined to turn that of the enemy, feveral half-fquadrons may be placed at quarter-diftance; at the ordered moment, the divifions of the column will wheel to the flank ranks by three's; the head of the leading divifion will take a new direction of the fame degree at which an incline is made; to this all the reft will, as foon as poffible, conform; and when they have opened about one hundred yards from the line, the leading half-fquadron will front, and move on a point taken fifty yards from the enemy's flank; the others continue their march rapidly by the flank, and paffing each other, they fucceffively front and move on beyond each other, the whole being thus at firft in an echellon to the rear, but which gradually changes to an echellon to the front, and at the finifhing of the attack, the enemy's flank and rear is gained.

———————

When flankers, fkirmifhers, or purfuers, are ordered out from the body of the fquadron, they may in general be taken from one or both flank divifions, and confift of one or two complete fub-divifions, or one or two complete three's, thereby leaving every other part of the fqua-dron entire; they will be commanded by appointed offi-cers, move out at the inftant of command, and proceed to perform thofe duties in which every cavalry foldier of every kind muft be individually inftructed and prac-tifed, and be mafter of the ufe of his fire-arms and fword, when fingle, as well as in rank.

———————

In a charge of either infantry or cavalry, though a momentary diforder may take place, yet the inftant the enemy gives way, the line muft be again formed, and the purfuit continued by light troops, or by detached troops or companies only. Thefe follow the enemy with the utmoft vigour, and as foon as the line is in order, it advances again and completes the defeat.

When

When cavalry attack infantry, they are apt to break, -but it ought always to be remembered, that when the enemy is difperfed, they give up the purfuit to the fecond line, which is fupported by the firft as foon as it regains its order. Light cavalry are in general placed in the fecond line.

When cavalry attack cavalry, the fquadrons muft be firm and compact ; but when they attack infantry, the files may be opened, and the men may bend down on their horfe's necks.

When cavalry attack infantry, they fhould in general do it in column ; and the fquadrons of the column fhould have at leaft three times as much diftance between them as the extent of their front. The leading fquadron after breaking the enemy's line, fhould move forward and form ; the two fucceeding ones fhould each wheel outwards by half fquadrons, and charge along the line ; whatever other fquadrons follow will fupport and act according to circumftances.

It may be expected, that under a fevere fire both the cavalry and infantry lofe to a degree their regular order, before they arrive on the enemy ; but cavalry acting againft cavalry, can profit by its manœuvre and order till the very laft moment; for, till the horfes heads come up againft each other, there is nothing that ought to prevent a cavalry foldier from being as fteady in the ranks, as if he was at a common exercife.

S. 51. *The Column of Route or March.*

The column of march is the foundation of all diftant movements, and even of evolutions and manœuvres.— It is in that manner that the columns of an army fhould perform their marches, that an enemy fhould be approached, and that fafety can be infured to the troops in their tranfitions from one point to another.

All marches, for any confiderable diftance, will at all
times

times be made preferably, where the ground allows, in column of divisions of the line, viz. by half squadrons, or divisions, or sub-divisions, when the squadrons exceed forty files.——But where the breadth of the routes so require it, the march will be made by ranks by three's or two's; or finally, by the filing of ranks; this last is never to be done but in cases of absolute necessity.

Whatfront made on.

All diminishing or increasing the front of a column of march, is in general done by each body of the column, at the point where the leading division first does it; such operation should be performed with quickness and firmness, so as if possible not thereby to retard or open out the column.—At all points of increasing or diminishing the front of the march, an intelligent officer should be stationed to see that it is performed with celerity; and the commander of a considerable column should have constant reports and inspections made, that the column is moving with proper regularity: he should have officers in advance to apprise him of difficulties to be avoided, or obstacles to be passed; and should himself apply every proper means to obviate such as may occur in the march.—The great principle, on all occasions, of diminishing or increasing the front of the column in march is, that such part as doubles, or forms up, shall slacken, or quicken its pace, as may be necessary to conform to the part which has no such operation to perform, but which continues its uniform march without the least alteration, as if no such process was going on; and if this is observed, distances can never be lost, or the column lengthened out.

Diminishing or increasing the front of the column.

Where a march is made near the enemy, if to a flank, the object must be, that at no time, if possible, the extent in column may be greater than the extent required in line; if to the front, or to the rear, then the object will be to march on a front of divisions, or half squadrons, with their distances closed up one half or more, that they may the more quickly deploy into a line when required; therefore, in such situations, if a column is obliged to diminish its front, from any obstacle in the route, it will, in general, after passing it, be ordered again to increase it,

March of the column near an enemy.

it, that it may be the better prepared for the great object of the march.

Attention of officers on the march.
On a march, there are so many occasional and temporary halts, that individual soldiers should at no other time be allowed to stop or dismount.—And when any of them are so permitted, it must be then evident, that the unavoidable halt will allow of this being done without affecting the march of the column.

No man must be permitted to ride in a careless lounging manner, which tends to fatigue and ruin the horse. —No one is to stop under pretence of watering his horse, much less is any division of the column to do so.— At a general halt, every necessary examination and adjustment of saddles, girths, &c. should be made.

Attention of commanding officers in column of march.
Regiments are not solely to depend on the one immediately before them for alteration of pace, or for the diminution or increase of the front of the column.—If there is reason to think that it has not originated from the front, they are to stop the mistake, and not continue it.——The look out of each commanding officer must be as forward as possible, at the same time that he is to recollect, in the execution of any of the operations of the column, how he can aid in moderating the difficulties and fatigue that always go on increasing to those behind him.

Change of direction.
The necessary changes in the direction of the route are gradually made by the divisions of the column, as on a moveable pivot, and not by quick and square wheels, unless the divisions are confined on each flank, and thereby obliged to make fixed wheels to prevent the loss of intervals.

Baggage.
On a march, servants, led horses, and canteen horses, remain with their squadrons.—The situation and movements of carriages belonging to the column, is prescribed in orders.

The place of the bat-horses is always ascertained for them, in the order in which their regiments follow each other: they are never to march in the divisions of the troops,

troops, but in front or rear of the whole column, according to circumftances, and as fhall be directed : a fufficient guard is to be with thofe of each regiment, and great care taken that they do not fall behind, ftraggle, or extend the column.

It is feldom that the bat-horfes can be ordered to march on the flank of the column; it ought only to be in ground where there is a certainty that no defile can occur, for in fuch cafe, they cannot be permitted to enter into the column, but muft ftop till the troops have paffed, and follow in rear.—When they do move on a flank, it is always on that flank which is not next the enemy.

.EVOLU-

EVOLUTIONS.

Divisions, from the Right march in Column to the Front.

A Caution.

Divisions!
  Right Wheel!
  March!
  Halt, Dress!
  March!
  Halt!

The divisions are wheeled to the right, except the first, which moves forward at the word march! to the left flank of the second division, and is there halted by its officer, who has shifted during the wheel (by the rear) for that purpose; at the word march, the whole move forward as far as necessary, and are there halted.*

Form Squadron on the Front Division by the Oblique march!

A Caution.

Divisions, right back, half wheel!
  March!
  Halt, Dress!
  March!
Left shoulder forward!
  Forward!
  Halt! Dress!

At this caution, the officers shift by the front, to the right of their divisions, and *halt, dress,* when the half wheel is completed: at the word march! they conduct them into line, giving the word, *left shoulder forward!* in proper time, so as to enable them to gain the half wheel required.

Columns of Divisions, from the left move off to the rear!

A Caution.

---

* If the squadron consists of 48 files, or upwards, the movement both to front and rear may be made by sub-divisions.

Divi-

DIVISIONS, LEFT WHEEL! MARCH! HALT, DRESS! MARCH! Left Wheel! Halt, Dress! March! The divifions *wheel* to the left, and at the fecond word, MARCH! the leading one again wheels to the left. The other divifions move on, and again feparately wheel to the left as they cover and follow in open column the leading divifion, which advances at fuch pace as is ordered.

ON THE LEADING DIVISION, TO THE REAR, FORM SQUADRON. The leading divifion by order wheels to the left about and *halts*. The others *wheel round* the *leading one*, and fucceffively join on its right. The officer bringing his divifion up in front of the left file, and then fhifting to his poft which his coverer has preferved.

FROM THE RIGHT OF HALF SQUADRONS TO THE FRONT, FILE. A Caution.

MARCH! The leaders of the rear rank move up to the front rank leaders, and both ranks file to the front from the named flanks, the ftandard leading the left half fquadron, the rear rank is the breadth of a horfe diftant from and dreffed to its front rank : quarter-mafter, &c. follow the files.——Leaders drefs, and preferve diftances from the left; commanding officer is with the ftandard half fquadron.

HALT! When fufficiently advanced, halt.

FRONT FORM SQUADRON. A caution immediately given.

The rear rank leaders cover the front rank leaders, who, with the ftandard, halt and are in a line.——
Each

MARCH!	Each rank forms up at the same time, file after file, to its proper leader, and looks to its formed flank; when the whole are up, the squadron will receive the word, center drefs! and correct any inaccuracy that may exift.
FROM THE LEFT OF HALF SQUADRONS TO THE REAR, FILE!	A caution—when one of the half fquadrons difengages by reining back.
MARCH!	The leaders turn to the rear, and the front rank leaders move up to the rear rank ones, the ftandard in front of its proper half fquadron (the right): quartermafters and trumpets follow their refpective half fquadrons. Leaders drefs and preferve diftances from the right.
TO THE REAR FORM SQUADRON!	The front rank leaders double round the rear rank leaders; place themfelves before them, and together with the ftandard halt.—Both ranks follow their leaders and form up at the fame time; when the whole are up, the fquadron will receive the word—*Center Drefs!*
FROM CENTER OF SQUADRON TO THE FRONT, FILE.	A Caution.
MARCH!	The ftandard, its coverer, and the four center files advance in front. The reft of the fquadron follow in file, till the whole is in four files: the commanding officer leads: the quarter mafter, &c. are in the rear;—dreffing and diftances

	{ tances are taken from the ftandards by the firft four men.
	The followers of the files attend to their leaders, at the fame time that each four may be dreffed to the right. The double files are feparated a horfe's breadth, if they cover their leaders.
HALT !	{ When the leader arrives at the intended line.
FRONT FORM SQUADRON.	} A Caution.
MARCH !	{ The ftandards and files on each fide of it ftand faft. The reft of the fquadron move up to their places, file by file, and drefs to the ftandard.

{ SQUADRONS, TO THE RIGHT WHEEL ! { MARCH !—HALT ! DRESS !	
{ SQUADRONS—RIGHT WHEEL ! { MARCH !—HALT ! DRESS !	
{ SQUADRONS—RIGHT ABOUT WHEEL ! { MARCH !—HALT ! DRESS !	Squadron Wheelings.
{ SQUADRONS—LEFT WHEEL ! { MARCH !—HALT ! DRESS !	
{ SQUADRONS—LEFT WHEEL ! { MARCH !—HALT ! DRESS !	
{ SQUADRON—LEFT ABOUT WHEEL ! { MARCH !—HALT ! DRESS !	

RETIRE IN LINE. HALT AND FRONT. }	Ranks by Three's.

The general commands are given by the chief of the whole; thofe of execution are repeated by leaders of fquadrons.

INSPEC-

INSPECTION, OR REVIEW OF A RE-
GIMENT OF CAVALRY.

The regiment marches to its ground in open column of fuch front as circumftances allow of—Forms on the alignement in clofe order, with intervals equal to one-third of the fquadron. Every individual is at his poft in fquadron, the regiment takes open order in the manner directed. The trumpets affemble on the right of the regiment in two ranks; and the ftaff, &c. of chaplain, furgeon, mate, are on the right of the trumpets in the line of the front rank, one horfe's length from it, and half a horfe from each other.

In this difpofition, and eyes to the right, the general is awaited. He is to be received with the compliment due to his rank, as fet forth in the regulations of military honours. On this occafion the fenior officers are at the head of fquadrons, and the commanding officer of the regiment is one horfe's length before the center of the whole.

A point is to be originally marked, about one hundred and fifty yards in front of the center of the regiment, where the general is fuppofed to take his ftation. But although he may choofe to quit that pofition, ftill that fpot is to be confidered as the point to work upon, and to which all movements and formations are relative.

Receiving the General.

DRAW SWORDS !

When the reviewing general prefents himfelf before the center, or before any part of the regiment (or line) the whole DRAW SWORDS, at three motions, the officers coming down at the laft motion to the pofition of the falute, in which fituation

ation they make a fufficient paufe, and then recover it with the commanding officer. During this operation the whole of the trumpets found, according to the rank of the general, and ftandards only falute fuch perfons, as from rank and regulation, are entitled to that honour.

The general then goes towards the right, (accompanied by the commanding officer) and the whole remain fteady, without paying any further compliment while he paffes along the regiment, during which time mufic will play or trumpets found, and they will ceafe when the general has returned to the right flank of the regiment, and is going away from it.

EYES LEFT.

When the general turns the left of the left fquadron, and paffes betwixt the ranks, that fquadron turns eyes to the left, as does each of the others, as he approaches them.

EYES RIGHT!
SLOPE SWORDS!

When the general is going from the regiment, each fquadron dreffes to the right, and flopes fwords.

REAR RANK,
TAKE CLOSE
ORDER!
RCH!

While the general is proceeding to place himfelf in the front, this command will be given, and the regiment prepares to march paft. On this particular occafion the officers will be cautioned not to alter their fituations, but to remain as at ORDER.

Marching paft.

The general having taken his pofition, the regiment is ordered to

G   wheel

THREE'S RIGHT WHEEL! MARCH! HALT, DRESS!	wheel to the right, ranks by three's : all the officers, &c. face to the right, and each as in a line of a rank of fixes. Trumpeters wheel into one rank, and the ftaff of furgeon, chaplain, &c. do not march paft.
MARCH!	To the flank, and in the continuation of the former front, which is marked accordingly.
RIGHT SHOULDERS FORWARD! FORWARD!	When the head of the regiment is about two hundred yards from where its center ftood, it will be led circling on a moveable pivot into a new direction, and march down perpendicular to the line on which it is to pafs the general, the head of each fquadron changing direction where the front one does.
HALF SQUADRON! HALT! WHEEL UP! HALT, DRESS! MARCH! EYES RIGHT! TAKE ORDER!	When the head of the leading fquadron arrives within five yards of the line on which it is to pafs the general, the feveral words to form the right half of that fquadron, and drefs to the right, are given rapidly and fucceffively: officers, trumpets and men front, and when the half fquadron has moved on twenty yards, the command is given to take order; the trumpets nimbly move forward, and place themfelves in two ranks before the commanding officer, and found a march. The farriers are a horfe's length behind the center of their troops, and the quarter-mafters behind the farriers.

In this manner, each half fquadron clears the ground for its fucceeding one, which performs the fame operation preparatory to paffing.

When

of the troops have, in the fame manner, filed paft, formed up, and are clofed up in its rear in column, at quarter diftance.

MARCH!

Juft before the rear troops have clofed up, and fo as that the laft one may not make any unneceffary paufe on the ground, the leading one will be put in motion, and each fucceffively will follow it in open column, when it acquires its proper diftance.

Left Wheel !
Halt, Drefs !
March !
Left Wheel !
Halt, Drefs !
March !

The leading half fquadron will wheel to the left, and proceed to the flank of the ground on which the line is to form ; it will there again wheel to the left, and march in the alignement, till it arrives at the right flank of the ground followed by the others in open column.

HALT !
WHEEL INTO
LINE !
MARCH !
HALT, DRESS !

The whole will then be ordered to halt and wheel into line.

Should a regiment not be directed to file paft, it will, after paffing by half fquadrons, enter the alignement, and form upon it.

SLOPE SWORDS !

In general fwords will be carried with the blade refting on the hollow of the fhoulder, and by the word SLOPE SWORDS ! On other ordered occafions, and in parade they will be carried upright at the word CARRY SWORDS !

CARRY SWORDS !

The

The regiment being now formed on their original ground, about one hundred and fifty yards from the general, will prepare to perform the fword exercife as follows:

SWORD EXERCISE.

1ſt, *The Six Diviſions in Line.*

2d, *The Six Diviſions in Speed.*

3d. *The Attack and Defence in Speed.*

The fword exercife performed in line, will be executed by the whole regiment, and the other movements by only one diviſion from each fquadron.

The Six Diviſions in Line.

It is not neceſſary herein to fpecify the words of command requiſite to be given, in order to put a regiment through the exercife; as the opening of ranks and doubling of files, are according to the mode laid down in the drill practice, and the whole being executed by flugelman, the commanding officer will have only to particularize each diviſion of movement, after which he will form up the doubling files, and clofe ranks.

The Six Diviſions in Speed.

DIVISIONS TO THE FRONT FORM. { The ranks being clofed, the diviſions are to be performed by thofe men who are previouſly appointed in each fquadron, moving forward on the word march, forming at three horfes' length in front of their refpective fquadrons, and dreſſing by the right.

In order to perform the exercife in fpeed, it will be requiſite to form the four diviſions in two lines, on each flank

flank of the regiment, with the whole fronting inwards. The two divifions of the left wing will be drawn up oppofite to the intervals of the divifion, upon the right and one fubaltern will accompany each divifion. The range between the two lines fhould not be lefs than one hundred and fifty yards, and the diftances of the divifions fufficiently great, to guard againft any poffibility of the oppofing parties riding againft each other.

RANKS BY THREE'S WHEEL OUTWARDS.

MARCH!

HALT! DRESS!
MARCH! TROT!

{ The divifions being formed in front of the line and told off in ranks by three's, the commanding officer will direct them to wheel outwards, and upon the word march, the two divifions of the right wing will wheel to the right, and thofe of the left in the oppofite direction. As foon as they are halted, they will again get the words march and trot, on which they will trot off beyond the flanks of the regiment, and wheel into their new alignement.

WHEEL UP!
HALT! DRESS!

{ As each divifion arrives on its ground, it is to halt, and wait for the commanding officer's order to wheel up.

When thus formed, the divifion of the third fquadron will be oppofite the interval of the two right divifions, with the fourth divifion upon its left.

PERFORM THE SIX
DIVISIONS OF
MOVEMENTS IN
SPEED.

{ On receiving the caution to perform in fpeed, the right and left file of the front rank will move forward a horfe's length in front of their refpective divifions, to be in readinefs to fpring forward upon the divifion being fpecified, at the fame time the flanks are to be kept complete by paffaging from the center of the rank.

The

FIRST DIVISION. {
The advanced files of each division will have, their horfes well in hand, and at the word DIVISION, move forward at an eafy gallop, increafing their fpeed gradually; each file is to direct his horfe in a right line to the front.

Thofe of the right wing, on arriving at the extremity of the range, will form to the rear of the third and fourth divifions, whilft thofe of the left wing will form in the intervals; by which means when the exercife is completed, the four divifions will be immediately oppofite each other.

Attention muft be paid to regulate the time requifite between each motion, according to the extent of ground, as every divifion of movement fhould begin and conclude at the oppofite extremity of the range.

The whole are executed according to the directions given for performing the firft divifion.

The Attack and Defence in Speed.

The attack and defence in fpeed, will confift of divifions filing fucceffively paft the general; the front and rear files attacking and defending alternately, which having done, they will return by the rear of the regiment to their places in fquadron.

On receiving the order to attack and defend in fpeed; the firft divifion of the right wing will file from its left by two's, the rear file commencing the attack on the front file, according to the mode pointed out in drill practice.

They are to move at a pace, rather exceeding half fpeed, taking care to ride in a right line to the oppofite end of the range, where the attack will ceafe; their fwords are immediately to be floped, the files to drefs, and at a gentle trot, wheel round the right flank of the regiment,

regiment, to their places in fquadron. The files will fucceed each other at the diftance of five horfes' lengths, till both divifions of the right wing have fucceffively rode paft the general.

Attention muft be paid that they all move off from the fame ground, which is pointed out by the leading files.

LEFT WING, BY YOUR RIGHT, ATTACK AND DEFEND.	The divifions of the left wing will file off from the right, and are in their turns to obferve the rules laid down for the divifions preceding, with this difference, that as their courfe is to be left, they will wheel round the left wing of the regiment to their places in fquadron.

The regiment remains formed at clofe order, ready for evolutions, movements or attacks, as ordered.

Whatever part of the evolutions are performed, they muft be arranged fo as to follow each other with propriety on the ground before the reviewing general.

Evolutions.

PLATE I

Reviewing Officer

Commanding Officer

Squadron Officer

Squadron Officer

Squadron Officer

Squadron Officer

F. Rank
R. Rank

Serefile and Supernumerary Officers.

Engraved by E.J. Smith, 69 Strand.

A REGIMENT is formed for exercise at close order. Squadron officers are a horse's length in front of the standard, supernumerary officers and serjeants, quarter-masters and trumpeters, are in the rear of the troops, in a line, at two horses distance from the rear rank, and their business is to attend to the movements of the squadron, and particularly to the rear rank.

MOVEMENTS AND ATTACKS.

1. The line is formed about one hundred yards from the general.

The open column of divisions trots past the general, and again forms in line on the ground it quitted. { The column of divisions is formed by the wheeling back of divisions. The column passes and takes up its ground at a trot. The flank leaders do not quit the pivot flanks, but they may order their divisions to turn their eyes to the right during the instant of passing.

Change

Plate II.

Change of Position on the left Flank, by throwing back the Right the Eighth of the Circle.

2. IN the change of position from A to B, the left half squadron of position A is wheeled by its leader into the new alignement B, which alignement is given by the mounted figures 1, 2.

The other half squadrons are in the mean time put about by three's, and the commanding officer wheels them to the right, in the degree requisite. During which the alignement B is prolonged by the markers of squadrons, who successively arrive at, and place themselves on the new alignement, which is terminated by marker 3.

Vide Section 43.

The round dots shew the posts of half squadron leaders, and the blunted arrows denote the markers of the wheel in echellon, as represented by figure F. The dotted lines shew the march of the leaders, and the pointed arrow the front to which they move.

The echellon G is the distance where each division is, in its turn, wheeled into the new direction, by bringing the left shoulders forward. As each half squadron arrives on the new line, it halts, fronts, and dresses.

The mounted figures are the squadron markers, who prolong the line, and place themselves on the outward flanks of their respective squadrons.

Squadron officers correct the line from the left flank.

PLATE II

PLATE III

Change of Pofition in Open Column, the *Left thrown back.*

Plate III.

3. THE pofition A is the fame which terminated the manœuvre No. 2, and B is the new alignement to be taken up.

EXAMPLE.

The commanding officer breaks the line A, into a column of divifions from the right, as reprefented in column F. When the column is put in motion, marker No. 1 turns the head of the column to the left.

Marker No. 2 directs it again to the left, and the marker No. 3 prolongs the line of the new direction B.

The firft fquadron having arrived on the alignement B, the column is halted.

The remaining three fquadrons G G G are wheeled by the commanding officer, ranks by three's to the right, and the leaders of divifions, fhifting at the fame time to that flank, will, at the word *march*, conduct their divifions into the column O, where they halt and front them, and from whence they are afterwards wheeled to the left into pofition B. Vide Section 17.

The blunt arrows in column F give the fquare of the wheel; the fmall arrows in column O are the markers of divifions fent out to take up the direction in the new column.

The markers for wheeling into the line B are reprefented by blunt arrows on the flanks of fquadrons.

The column O being wheeled into line, the fquadron officers will fhift to the left flank, and drefs their fquadron from that point.

Change

Plate IV. *Change of Position on the Right Flank, the Left brought forward.*

4. THE position A is the same which terminated the manœuvre No. 3, and B is the new alignement to be taken up.

The right half squadron of position A is wheeled by its leader into the new direction B, which alignement is taken up by the markers 1, 2. The remaining half squadrons are by the commanding officer wheeled to the right in the degree requisite, as represented by the echellon F. The leaders will then shift to the inward flank, and at the word *march!* move forward to the position B, the squadron markers taking care at the same time to advance at an encreased pace, in order to prolong the alignement, which is terminated by the marker 3.

Vide Section 43.

The echellon G denotes the wheeling of half squadrons into the alignement B, by bringing the left shoulders forward.

Squadron officers will dress their squadrons from the right.

The

PLATE IV

PLATE V

The cloſe Column is formed, marches and deploys into Line.

Plate V.

5. IN plate No. 5, there are three movements, as diſtinguiſhed by the initials **I. L. M.** The firſt movement **(I)** conſiſts in forming a column behind the left half ſquadron; the ſecond movement **(L)** repreſents the flank march of the column to the right. In the third movement **(M)** the column deploys, and forms line on a central half ſquadron.

On movement **(I)**, the line A being ordered by the commanding officer to form cloſe column to the rear of the left half ſquadron, the left half ſquadron officer will place the marker No. 1. The line is then wheeled by half ſquadrons, an eighth to the left (half ſquadron No. 7. excepted, which diſengages by reining back.) The whole will afterwards take ground by three's to the left, when the leaders placing themſelves at the heads of their half ſquadrons, are, at the word *march!* to conduct them to the places in column, where they will cover and dreſs to the right. *Vide Section.*

No markers are neceſſary to regulate the diſtance of half ſquadrons in cloſe column.

Movement L. The column B is wheeled by the commanding officer, ranks by three's to the right, and marched till it arrives oppoſite the general, when he will order it to halt and wheel up. During its flank march, guides are to be ſent out, to direct the movement of the column parallel to its proper front. *Vide Section 33.*

Movement M. A caution being given, to deploy on a central half ſquadron, the officer of the named half ſquadron ſends markers, No. 1, 2, to determine the ground occupied by the front half ſquadron, to which he will march whenever his front is clear. *Vide Section 37. Example 3.*

The commanding officer will then direct the half ſquadrons to wheel outwards by three's; that on which the deployment is made ſtands faſt, thoſe to its front wheel

wheel to the left, and thofe in the rear to the oppofite hand.

The officers fhifting to the heads of their half fquadrons will at the word *march !* lead ftraight out, and as each half fquadron arrives parallel to the ground where it is to form on the new line, it will halt, wheel up, and move forward into line.

Squadron markers are to prolong the line as ufual, and officers will drefs their fquadrons from the flank to which they formed.

Counter-

PLATE VI

Countermarch of the Divisions of the Open Column.

Plate VI.

6. IN the annexed plate there are two figures, L and M. L reprefents the line A, broken into a column of divifions, right in front, which column marches the diftance of a fquadron's length. M reprefents the countermarch of divifions.

On movement L. In wheeling by divifions, the ufual markers for each fquadron give the fquare of the wheel, and when in column, the covering and dreffing is to the left.

Movement M. The fquadrons 1, 2, 3, 4, of column G, are required to countermarch; and on the commanding officer giving a caution to that effect, a marker, from the right of each divifion, will immediately go to the left flank, and occupy the officer's place in the divifion, with this difference, that he turns his horfe *to the front intended by the countermarch*, (vide the markers in column G) the officer at the fame time fhifts to the right of the divifion, and at the word *March!* the divifion files from the right, and is conducted by the rear to the marker on the oppofite flank, when it receives from the divifion officer the words *Form, Drefs.* The column being formed to the new front, it returns to its former ground, covering and dreffing to the right.

Vide Section 27.

In all countermarches by files, the divifion officer will lead out to the flank, in the degree of one third the front of his divifion, before he countermarches.

H

The

Plate VII. *The open Column changes Pofition to the Flank, by the Flank March of its Divifions.*

7. THE column G retires by a flank march of its divifions; it then halts in the pofition of column F, and wheels into the line A.

Vide Section 21.

The column G having received a caution to retire, the divifions will be wheeled by three's to the left, at which time the leaders are to fhift by the rear to the head of their divifions, and at the word *March!* retire conducted by the divifion on the right. When arrived at the diftance of two hundred yards from the former ground, the column will be ordered to halt, and wheel up, on which the divifions will wheel by three's to the right; the leaders are then to return to the right flank, to which hand they muft cover and drefs, ready to wheel into the line A. During the retreat, great attention is to be paid, that the leaders of the divifions drefs, and wheeling intervals are properly preferved, from the *right divifion*, it being the head divifion of the column when fronted. When the markers 1, 2, are placed, and the caution given to wheel into line, thofe who direct the fquare of the wheel immediately aligne themfelves on the points thrown out for that purpofe; and at the word *March!* the divifions will come rapidly into line, and the officers drefs their fquadrons from the right flank.

Attack

PLATE VII

PLATE VIII

North sculp. Edward

8. THE line A attacks to the front, by fquadrons from the right; each moving when the one preceding it has juft finifhed its attack. They fucceffively arrive and halt in line.

The adjutant places himfelf in the pofition of marker No. 1, on whom the right fquadron officer will lead his fquadron to the charge, which having made, the adjutant will fhift to the front of the fecond fquadron for the fame purpofe, and fo fucceffively be- Vide Sec-come the point of direction for each fquadron officer. tion 9.

After the charge is completed, flank ferjeants (markers 3, 4,) turn out to drefs the fquadron, which is done from the center.

The

Plate IX. *The Line retires in Echellon.*

9. THE line A retires in echellon of fquadrons from the left, and afterwards forms the line B, on the right center fquadron.

The commanding officer having given the caution to retire in echellon, of fquadrons from the left, the left fquadron officer will put his fquadron about by three's, and lead in a right line to the rear. As foon as the left fquadron is arrived at the diftance of thirty yards from the line A, the left center fquadron will march; and in like manner, are the other fquadrons to move in echellon. When the retreat is made in the degree required, the whole will be halted, and receive orders to form the line on the right center fquadron, which fquadron is inftantly fronted, and dreffed by the markers 1, 2.

Vide page 57.

The remaining fquadrons are conducted by their leaders into line (which line is fucceffively prolonged by the markers on the outer flanks of each fquadron, and terminated by the markers 3 and 4): The right fquadron moves up and fronts on the new line, and the two left fquadrons inftantly come about, and move forward to their markers. As each fquadron arrives on the new line, the officers drefs their fquadrons on the firft formed fquadron.

The

PLATE IX

A

B

1

2

3

4

A

B

C

PLATE X

10. THE line A advances to the charge. B is the Vide Sec- poſition to which it charges, and C the alignement tion 45. taken up after the charge is made.

The line A advances to the charge, and the right center ſquadron being named as the ſquadron of di-rection, it muſt be the particular care of its leader to move on in a direct line to his front ; and in order to preſerve that uniformity of motion, which inſures a ſteady charge, he muſt gradually increaſe his pace, till he arrives at the charge in ſpeed.

The line is halted by the commanding officer on the poſition B, and if a correct dreffing is required, markers 1 and 2 move forward from the ſquadron of direction, and take up the alignement C, which is immediately prolonged by the markers of the other ſquadrons. Each ſquadron moves up as its reſpective markers are placed, and dreffes on the ſquadron of direction.

Should the next movements not be performed, the line will retire after the charge, about one hundred yards, ranks by three's, then halt, front, advance at open order, and general ſalute.

Plate XI. *The Line retires, and forms two Columns.*

11. THE annexed plate reprefents three figures, diftinguifhed by the letters I, L, M. Part of the line I, forms a column of half fquadrons, behind the adjoining half fquadron, at quarter diftance.

L reprefents the retiring of the line; and in M is feen the clofing up of the column, and the two left half fquadrons formed behind their adjoining one.

On movement I. The two fquadrons on the right having been cautioned to form a column of half fquadrons, at quarter diftance, behind the adjoining half fquadron H, the marker 1, is to be immediately placed; the commanding officer will then wheel the right wing by half fquadrons an eighth to the left, and afterwards by three's to the fame hand.

The leaders will place themfelves at the head of their half fquadrons, and at the word *march!* conduct them into column, where they are to cover and drefs by the right.

Movement L. When the column is formed, the whole will be put about by three's, and retire to the pofition L, where the commanding officer will halt and front them.

Movement M. The column L having fronted, it will be ordered to clofe to the front, as reprefented in figure M. The left fquadron is then wheeled by half fquadrons, an eighth to the right, and afterwards take ground by three's to the right, when at the word *march!* they will be conducted into column, behind the adjoining half fquadron B, where they are to cover and drefs to the left.

PLATE XI

PLATE XII

12. THE column A deploys, during which the Vide Sec-
front fquadron C moves forward; the left fquadron tion 50.
forms to the front, whilft the two fquadrons on the
right take the oblique direction G, from whence the
whole will charge to the pofition B, the movements of
the front attack correfponding with that of the flank.

The column having received a caution to attack in
front and flank, the adjutant will place himfelf oppofite the right flank of the column, in the fituation of
marker No. 1. The commanding officer then wheels
half fquadrons by three's outwards, which having done,
at the word *march!* the whole will move together. The
formed fquadron C moves forward. Half fquadrons
7, 8, deploy and form fquadron M, dreffing by the
right. Half fquadrons 1, 2, 3, 4, compofing the right
wing, lead in the oblique direction G; when having
gone one hundred yards, or more, the leading half
fquadron 4, wheels up and dreffes, fo as to be nearly
perpendicular to its charging point marker 1; it then
advances, and the other half fquadrons, 3, 2, 1, proceed to the flank, and fucceffively halt, wheel, and
come up to the right of each other; during which,
the movements of the left wing (fquadrons C and M)
are carried on, and made to correfpond to this flank
attack.

H 4   *Retire*

Retire in two Lines by alternate Half Squadrons.

13. THE regiment A A retires by alternate half fquadrons in two lines, to pofition B, and during the retreat, the half fquadrons of the right wing gradually gain their pofition in line.

Vide Section 47. The regiment is cautioned to retire in two lines. The right half fquadrons (1, 3, 5, 7,) to compofe the firft line.

The fecond line ftands faft. The firft line is put about by three's, and at the word *march!* will retreat towards the pofition B, dreffing by a named half fquadron.

The retiring line having marched a given diftance, will receive orders to *halt!* and *front!* which orders ferve as a fignal to the fecond line to begin its retreat, in the fame manner, through its proper intervals.

The alternate retreat is thus continued, till the line has attained the pofition B.

14. GENERAL SALUTE.

REAR ranks are opened, and the regiment advances in parade order, trumpets founding, &c. &c. within thirty yards of the general.

HALT!

GENERAL SALUTE.

PLATE XIII

ADDITIONAL INSTRUCTIONS.

The evolutions, movements and attacks are fuch as feem effential for the general practice of the regiment. The whole of them may not be required at any one exercife or infpection, and fuch therefore as are to be performed (always including the firft feven movements if fpace allows), muft be arranged and connected according to the extent of, and circumftances of the ground on which they are to be exhibited; and on the fmalleft fpot fuch changes of pofition may be made, as will clearly fhew what may be expected from the body in more extended fituations.

No improper paufes fhould be made betwixt the connected parts of the fame movement. The detached points neceffary in formations fhould be timeoufly prepared and given by the perfons who are fo ordered.

Commanding officers are moveable according to circumftances, and fhould by no means confider the center as their general poft in exercife or movements, or expect by the exertion of one voice, from one fixed fituation, to command and direct the whole; their prefence is more frequently required near one or other flank; in general they fhould be at the conducting point of movement, or formation, and to that addrefs their orders by voice or meffage, for if that point be led, or placed in the direction it fhould take, there is little danger of the parts of the body, not properly, and fucceffively conforming to it.

The words of command as marked in the margin and thofe at the end of the book, for the movements, are to be ftrictly made ufe of, and no other fubftituted in their room; in the quick movements, and manœuvres of cavalry they muft be rapidly given.

In

In paffing by in half-fquadrons at open ranks, the commander of the fquadron will be in front of his leading half-fquadron, covered by the ftandard with which the other officers of the half-fquadron drefs. In the fecond half-fquadron all its officers are in front, and in one line. The trumpets are all in front of the regiment, and when they have paffed, wheel quickly round, and remain pofted oppofite his Majefty, and found till the regiment has paffed, when they ceafe.

In paffing by half-fquadrons or divifions, at clofe ranks, the ftandard may take the center of the front rank of the leading one. The commanding officer is before it, other officers are at their fquadron-pofts, and care is taken that there fhall be an officer on each paffing flank.

At the drawing of fwords, and general falute, on his Majefty's approach, the trumpets all found the parade march. When his Majefty paffes along the line, the regiment founds its own march, or fuch other as fhall be ordered.

The trumpet flourifh, in drawing fwords, is ufed regimentally on their own ground, and is the founding ufed in receiving a major-general ; it is repeated twice for a lieutenant-general, and to all fuperior generals the march is founded.

In parade, to receive his Majefty, or the commanding general, the trumpets are affembled on the right of their regiments in two ranks, and the ftaff beyond them. The ftaff does not march paft.

On all occafions of exercife and manœuvre, trumpets are behind their troops and fquadrons, unlefs otherwife detached.

In general, a regiment fhould manœuvre before the
perfon

perfon infpecting it, fo as to terminate many of its movements and formations within twenty or thirty yards of where he ftands.

SKIRMISHING.

Skirmifhers, or ranks detached to fire, fhould be at leaft two hundred yards from the fquadron, if the ground allows.

When any part of the fquadron is detached to attack, or fire, the remainder always fupport with drawn fwords.

The ftandard always remains with the body of the fquadron, and never moves with any detached part of it. Single fkirmifhers can take the fureft aim, with their carbines, to the left; they will alfo occafionally fire to the front, and to the right; but muft take the greateft care not to hit, or burn the horfe's head, or at that time to fpur him.

Skirmifhers fhould always retire in proportion as the fquadron retires; cover the front of it, at one hundred and fifty yards diftance at leaft, and manage fo as to keep up a conftant fire, nor fhould they ever remain in a clufter to become a mark. All firings are beft performed on the move; and it is unneceffary to halt for that purpofe only. Whenever the line retires, fkirmifhers fhould be ordered out to cover the retreat, and fhould join at the firft fignal. No fkirmifhers ever to fire but when advanced to the front, and never when behind other men. Skirmifhers if not ordered to join, retire through the intervals when the line advances to charge; and form and fupport. The retreat of the line fhould be generally made at a brifk pace; to get quick off the ground, and no time ought to be loft in giving the proper fignal, or word of command. In detached open ranks, the officer commanding the rank is always moft conveniently placed in the center of it, and the men drefs and are directed by him.

Skirmifhers

Skirmiſhers are to be very attentive and alert in inſtantly obeying the ſignals made for their direction, particularly thoſe of ceaſing to fire, and of rallying to their
diviſions : and when the ſignal for calling in ſkirmiſhers
is ſucceeded by that of rally made from the main body,
the diviſions themſelves return quickly, even though
they ſhould not then be joined by their detached men.

Skirmiſhing detachments are uſually made of a flank
diviſion or ſub-diviſion (or their front or rear ranks
only) of ſquadrons. *In advancing,* theſe are rapidly
ſent forward about one hundred and fifty yards in front
of their reſpective ſquadrons, from which *body* are detached three or more *files,* one hundred yards ſtill further
forward, where they halt fronting the enemy. The
outward flank files of this advanced detachment ſtand
faſt, while the others file inwards towards each other, in
order to divide the ground and cover the front of the re-
ſerve as well as that of their ſquadron.

This operation, followed by all the detachments from
the ſquadrons, will effectually cover the front of a corps.

In this ſituation the advanced line of ſkirmiſhers are to
have their piſtols or carbines at the recover ; (if piſtols,
then the ſword is to be ſlung to the wriſt). The rear
rank men will invariably cover thoſe of the front rank ;
while the front rank advances in ſkirmiſhing.

When the front rank has fired, the rear rank is
brought forward in its turn, by the officer or ſerjeant
who is ſtationed between the two lines, in order to ſee
and direct the rear one. The advancing line will regulate its pace by his, and will halt and dreſs by him when
he halts.

For this movement of the rear line to the front, the
officer or ſerjeant commanding gives the word, *Rear
rank forward!* accompanied by a wide ſignal with his
ſword ; the rear rank paſſes the front line fifty yards,
when the rear rank begins to load.

The files of the front line muſt attend particularly to
the circumſtance of not firing till the rear line (their
ſupport), is loaded. On this principle will each rank
paſs

pafs through the other, fucceffively firing and fupporting each other. Each man of the front rank, either in advancing or retiring, will pafs his rear rank man to his right, whilft the rear rank men under the fame circumftances pafs on the left. This regulation prevents any two men paffing through the fame interval.

In retiring. When the rank next the enemy has fired, it retires by word of command, affifted by fignal, and forms fifty yards in rear of thofe by whom they were before covered, and as they front immediately begin to load. The inftant the retiring line has paft the fupporting line, the fkirmifhers make a flank movement to each hand for a few paces and back again, in order not to be fixed marks for the enemy's fkirmifhers : at the fame time they are occafionally to halt and fire as they perceive their rear file loaded. Thus the two lines retire through each other fucceffively fronting and fupporting. ——To retire, the word of command is, *about !*—to face the enemy, *Front!*—In retiring, each file turns his horfe to the left about :—in fronting he brings him to the right about :

Whenever fkirmifhers are called in they form to the referve, returning their piftols and floping their fwords, without waiting for any word of command to do fo.— The officer commanding the divifion puts the divifion about by three's, and returns to his place in fquadron. But fhould the line be advancing to the charge, the divifions, if they can, will gain their place in fquadron and join in the charge; or otherwife they will form behind the fquadron and fupport.

When a line or column moves to a flank, and that fkirmifhers are out, they are not to wait an order for them to conform to that movement of the main body, but will cover that flank which may be expofed to the enemy; for inftance : if the movement of the line is to the right, then the left of the line of march muft be covered; and the reverfe is to be obferved in the oppofite cafe.

The fkirmifhers covering a flank movement will march in fingle file, the rear rank man immediately behind his front rank file, judging the diftance fo as completely to cover the fquadron, which fhould be out-
flanked

flanked by its fkirmifhers rather than otherwife. The fame principle of referving the fire with the front line, till the rear fupport is loaded, muft equally be attended to in flank movements, as in the cafes of advancing or retiring; but in the practice there is this difference, that a front file in a flank movement cannot fee when his referve has loaded, therefore it is to be announced to him by word, *Ready!* when he will fire at difcretion.

Advanced guards and patroles on the flanks, are in all fituations effential to guard againft a furprize, and the ftrength of both muft depend upon that of the body in march, and other circumftances. Although in general, the movement of an army is fo covered by light troops, and advanced corps, that every other precaution feems unneceffary; yet no column or detached body is to neglect this military precaution for its peculiar fafety; and the conduct of the advanced guard of an officer and forty or fifty men, may fhew the general principles on which more confiderable bodies are to act on the fame fervice.

The advanced guard in general marches about two hundred yards in front of the column, regiment, or fmaller body; but the diftance muft depend on the nature of the country, which, when woody, makes it neceffary to remain nearer the main body, than when it is free from inclofures.

From the advanced guard, the officer detaches to his front a ferjeant and twelve men, who are to preferve the fame diftance from the officer's party, that the officer is from the column.

The ferjeant is in like manner to fend two men forward, and detach two others, one on each flank, as fide patroles, who are to keep in a line with thofe men moft in advance. The officer will for the fame purpofe, detach one non-commiffioned officer and four men on each of his flanks. The fide patroles are diftant between three and four hundred yards on the flanks, which diftance varies according to the places they have to examine, and the impediments met with on the march:
they

they are not to lofe fight of each other for any length of time, but to take the advantage of every height to look round them, and fee that they preferve a correfponding line with each other, and the march of the advanced guard.

The patroles muft examine all villages, hollow ways, and woods, that lie in the direction of their march, taking care to reconnoitre from the heights the country below, before they defcend into the vallies. As foon as the enemy is perceived, the perfon who difcovers him muft fire a piftol to announce it, when the non-commif-fioned officer of the party will ride to the fpot, and having made his obfervations, fend a correct report of what he has feen to the officer, who is to convey it to the officer commanding the column.

It is a neceffary precaution to fend out fide patroles from the column, and likewife a rear guard when it is poffible for an enemy to approach in that direction. The rear guard is to be conducted on the fame principle directed for the advance.

_____

An out-poft having been taken up under a knowledge of the country, its *relief* will be conducted in the following manner :

When arrived at the poft, the relief takes place by drawing up behind the old guard, who muft be on horfeback to receive the new guard. The number of men neceffary for the relief of the videts (or fentries), are then to be marched off, and conducted by a non-commiffioned officer of the old guard.

The officers attend the relief, and the relieving officer muft inform himfelf of the particular orders of every videt; have pointed out to him how far the videts advance by day, and where retired to at night; whether the enemy appeared during the twenty-four preceding hours, and in what direction : he muft afk the names of the villages, and the direction of the roads, which he will compare on the fpot with his map : he fhould know what patroles have been made, to what diftance, and how frequent ; what pofts his flanks communicate

with ;

with; and in cafe of an attack, the fupport to be expected, and from what quarters : he likewife will inform himfelf of the name of the field officer commanding the line of pofts, and where he is to be found, in order to report to him if neceffary.

The Relief having been made, the new guard will take up the fame ground which the old one occupied.—The men may difmount, but not take off their accoutrements, or be permitted to ftray from their horfes.

The horfes are to be kept conftantly bitted, except when feeding, which muft never exceed one fourth of the number at a time, and at fuch hours as the enemy are leaft likely to appear.

No perfon is to be allowed to pafs the out-poft without producing an order from the general commanding in chief; nor is any perfon to be permitted to approach the guard, under a pretence of felling provifions, or for any other purpofe, without the officer firft being informed of it.

The officer muft vifit his videts frequently by day, and keep conftant patroles moving by night. The appearance of any enemy in force, their approach by night, or the defertion of any of the videts with the watchword, muft not only be immediately communicated to the field officer commanding, but to the pofts on the right and left, and the *counterfign* be changed to guard againft furprize.

Before fun fet, if not done in the early part of the day, the officer fhould reconnoitre in front of his poft ; for which purpofe he muft determine from his map the route to be taken, and with fifteen or twenty of his guard, he will advance on the fame principle of caution pointed out for an advanced guard ; only that the party muft be concentrated, the force being lefs confiderable and unfupported. An officer on out-poft duty fhould be provided with a good glafs, which, in reconnoitring, will always be found very ferviceable. Wherever two roads meet, the party fhould halt, till one of the roads is reconnoitred,

reconnoitred, without which it cannot be fafe to proceed on the other.

On duties of patrole or reconoitring parties, the men muft be filent and watchful, and march at open files.

At night, patroles are to be conducted in fmaller bodies than reconnoitring parties; they will direct their march on the different roads leading towards the enemy. Three men are to be advanced in front of the patrole, two of whom may be a hundred yards, and the third man fifty more, in front of them. A caution always requifite to be taken to guard againft furprize.

A non-commiffioned officer, or junior officer, generally conducts the patrole, as the officer commanding muft not leave his guard during the night.

The utmoft filence is neceffary to the fafety of a patrole, and that they fhould march with files very open. The barking of dogs in villages occupied by the enemy, moving of lights, or any noife breaking in on the ftillnefs of the night, are tokens of the enemy being in motion, and to which patroles muft direct their particular attention.

The guard will mount their horfes an hour before funfet, and continue fo till dark; likewife before daybreak, and remain mounted till the approach of an enemy may be clearly perceived, or that the relief arrives; which relief generally takes place at day-break, in order to have the guards doubled at the time moft dangerous for furprize.

TRUMPET

TRUMPET DUTY SOUNDINGS.

———

1. *Reveille*
2. *Stable Call*   For ſtable duties.
3. *Boots and Saddles*   { When to turn out on horſe-
4. *To Horſe*   back, for a march, exerciſe, or other duty.

5. *Draw Swords*   Theſe ſoundings begin at the inſtants of drawing the ſword
6. *Return Swords*   *from*, and returning it *to* the ſcabbard.

7. *Parade March*
8. *Parade Call*   For aſſembling on foot
9. *Officers Call*
10. *Serjeants Call*
11. *Trumpeters Call*
12. *Orders*
13. *Dinner Call*   For men, and for officers.
14. *Watering Call*   To turn out in watering order.
15. *Setting the Watch*

Theſe duty ſoundings, according to ſituation, are given by one trumpet, or by the whole of the quarter, regiment, or camp.

———

TRUMPET EXERCISE SOUNDINGS.

16. *March.*

> The fquadron, regiment or line, being halted, the trumpet of the commander will accompany the word, *The will advance*; and at the word *March*, the whole will move at a walk.

17. *Trot.*

18. *Gallop.*
19. *Charge.*

> When the body is marching at a walk, on the fignal to trot, the whole inftantly receive the word *Trot*, and change pace immediately. The fame is to be obferved from the trot to the light *Gallop*, and from the gallop to the *Charge*. During the charge itfelf, the trumpets of all the fquadrons that are charging, may found.

20. *Halt.*

> The whole halt on the word of command. After the halt of a retreating body, the proper command will bring it to its proper front.

21. *Retreat.*

> The fignal of *Retreat* (which will be often preceded by that of halt) is a general caution for the feveral words of execution to be given.

22. *Rally.*

> The fignal to *Rally* may be continued as long as it is neceffary, and be repeated by the trumpets of fuch parts of the body, as are concerned in the operation, till the end is anfwered.

Thefe fignals are given by the chief commander only of the whole body that is exercifed, whether of a fquadron, regiment, brigade, or a line; they are not repeated by other commanders; they are addreffed as cautions to the commanding officers of the parts of fuch

I 2.

body,

body, not to the men, nor is any movement, or alteration of movement, to take place, but in confequence of
the words, *march, trot, gallop,* &c. &c. rapidly and
loudly repeated, the inftant the trumpet caution is given.

The fignals of movement are fo fhort, that the words
of execution may nearly coincide with them.

> Thefe fignals for quick move-
> ment, may in regular exercife be
> given by a perfon who at the in-
> ftant of giving them is ftationary;
> but if he leads the body in motion,
> it is evident that in the gallop, the
> charge, and the halt, the voice,
> and the eye, can only determine,
> and regulate.

---

23. *Turn out
Skirmifhers.*

> This fignal is made by the com-
> mander of the whole, if the whole
> is concerned, otherwife by the
> commander of fuch part only as is
> to execute; if one or two fqua-
> drons only, the voice will fuffice.
> It may be a fignal for purfuers
> after a charge.

24. *Call in Skir-
mifhers.*

> This fignal is made by the com-
> mander of the whole, and re-
> peated by the commander of de-
> tachments for the fkirmifhers to
> join their detachments; or it may
> originally come from the com-
> mander of the detachments. On
> the fignal to *rally,* the whole join
> the bodies they were detached
> from.

25. *Skirmifhers
ceafe firing.*

> This fignal is made by the com-
> mander of the whole, and repeated
> (or originally made) by the com-
> mander of the fupporting detach-
> ments, from which the fkirmifhers
> are advanced.

BUGLE

BUGLE HORN DUTY SOUNDINGS.

1. *Reveille*
2. *Roufe, or turn out*
3. *Dinner call*
4. *Setting the watch*

{ Thefe foundings are different in their notes from thofe
of the trumpet, but may be
ufed under the fame circumftances.

BUGLE HORN EXERCISE SOUND-
INGS.

5. *March*
6. *Trot*
7. *Gallop*
8. *Charge*
9. *Halt*
10. *Retreat*
11. *Rally*
12. *Turn out fkirmifhers*
13. *Skirmifhers ceafe firing*
14. *Call in fkirmifhers*

Thefe foundings are exactly
the fame as thofe of the
trumpet, in the place of
which the bugle horn
may be occafionally fub-
ftituted.

Thefe fignals of the trumpet and bugle horn are meant
in aid of the voice, but are by no means to be fubftituted
for, or prevent the *ordered* words of execution.

The trumpet is always to be confidered as the principal military inftrument for thefe foundings. It more
particularly belongs to the line, and the bugle horn to
detached parties.

I 3

WORDS

WORDS OF COMMAND.

Comm. Officer.	Squadron Officer.	Divifion Leaders.	The open Column of Divifions trots paſt the General, and again forms in line on the Ground it quitted.	Obfervations.
*	*		Divifions, left backward wheel!	(a) The line may be put threes about, wheeled forward by divifions, halt, front, and drefs.
*	*		March!	
		*	Halt! Drefs!	
*	*		March!	
		*	Left wheel! Forward!	
		*	Left wheel! Forward!	
		*	Eyes Right!	
		*	Carry Swords!	
		*	Slope Swords!	
		*	Eyes Left!	
		*	Left wheel! Forward!	
		*	Left wheel! Forward!	
*	*		Halt!	
*	*		Wheel into line!	
*	*		March!	
		*	Halt! Drefs!	
		*	Eyes Front!	

Conm. Officer.	Squadron Officer.	H. Squa. Officer.	Change of Pofition on Left Flank, Right thrown back.	Obfervations.
*	*		Threes about! March! (a)	(a) Left half fquadron officer wheels his half fquadron the half wheel into the new alignement.
	*		Halt! Drefs!	
*	*		Half fquadrons—Right quarter wheel! March!	
	*	*	Halt! Drefs!	
*	*	*	March!	
		*	Left fhoulders forward! Forward! Halt! Front! Halt! Drefs! March! Halt! Drefs!	

N. B. It is to be confidered as an invariable rule, that the caution and words of command, given by the commanding officer previous to every movement, are repeated by the fquadron officers to the utmoft extent of voice, without which no manœuvre can be executed with precifion, as a variety of cau-fes may prevent the commanding officer being heard where the line is extenfive.

Comm. Officer.	Squadron Officer.	H. Squa. Officer.	Divifion Leaders.	Change of Pofition in open Column, Left thrown back.	Obfervations.
*	*			Divifions—Right wheel! March!	
	*		*	Halt! Drefs!	
			*	Eyes Left!	
*	*			March!	
			*	Right fhoulders forward! Forward! (a)	(a) Repeated by divifion leaders on arriving at marker 1 and 2
*	*			Halt!—Rear divifions will march into the new direction. (b)	(b) The fquadron in the new alignement wheels into line.
				Threes, Right wheel! March!	
		*		Halt! Drefs!	
*	*			March!	
			*	Right fhoulders forward! Forward! Halt! Wheel up! Halt! Drefs! (c)	(c) Repeated by divifion leaders on arriving in the new direction.
*	*			Wheel into line! March!	
		*		Halt! Drefs! Eyes front!	

Comm. Officer.	Squadron Officer.	H. Squa. Officer.	*Change of Position on the Right Flank, Left brought forward.*	Observations.
*			Half squadrons—Right quarter wheel! March! (a)	
	*		Half squadrons—Right quarter wheel! March!	(a) Right half squadron officer wheels his half squadron into the new alignement.
		*	Halt! Drefs!	
*	*		March!	
		*	Left shoulders forward! Forward! Halt! Drefs! (b)	(b) Repeated in succession by half squadron officers.
	*		Eyes front!	

Comm. Officer.	Right Wing Squa. Officer.	Right Wing H.Sq. Officer.	Left Wing Squa. Officer.	Left Wing H.Sq. Officer.	*Clofe Column is formed on the Left Half Squadron, marches to its Right, and deploys into Line.*	Obfervations.
*	*		*		Form clofe column to the rear of the left half fquadron!— Half fquadron, Left eighth wheel! March!	
	*		*		Halt! Drefs!	
*	*		*		Three's left wheel! March!	
	*		*		Halt! Drefs!	
*	*		*		March!	
		*		*	Left fhoulders forward! Forward! Halt! Wheel up! Halt! Drefs! (a)	(a) Repeated fucceffively by half fquadron officers as they arrive in column.
*					Column—Three's right wheel! March! Halt! Drefs! March! Halt! Wheelup! Halt! Drefs!	
*					Fòrm line on the right center (or fifth) half fquadron—— Three's outward wheel!	
	*				Three's right wheel! ⎫ Repeated Three's left wheel! ⎭ together.	
			*		March! Halt! Drefs! March!	
*		*		*	Halt! Wheel up! Halt! Drefs! March! (b)	(b) Right wing marches (after wheeling up) by its left, and dreffes to that flank. Left wing marches and dreffes by its right.
					Eyes front!	

Comm. Officer.	Squadron Officer.	Divifion Leaders.	*The Line will countermarch in Column of Divifions.*	Obfervations.
*	*		Divifions—Right wheel! March	
	*	*	Halt! Drefs!	
		*	Eyes left!	
*	*		March! Halt! The divifions will countermarch!	
*	*		To the right file! March!	
		*	(*a*) Left fhoulders forward! Forward! Left form!	(*a*) The leading files wheel to the right about after leading out a fufficient diftance, to bring the left off its ground before the right arrives to form.

Comm. Officer.	Squadron Officer.	Divifion Leaders.	The Column will retire by a Flank March of Divifions.	Obfervations.
*	*		Threes left wheel! March!	
	*		Halt! Drefs!	
*	*		March! Halt! Wheel up!	
	*		Halt! Drefs!	
		*	Eyes right!	
*	*		Right wheel into line! March!	
	*		Halt! Drefs! Eyes front!	

Comm. Officer.	Squadron Officer.	The Line will attack by Squadrons from the Right.	Observations.
*	*	No. 1. March! Trot! Canter! Charge! Halt! (*a*) No. 2. No. 3. }Repeated in succession. No. 4.	(*a*) Flank markers are turned out (if necessary) by the squadron officer placing himself in the center, and aligning with the serjeant, he moves the squadron up.

Comm. Officer.	Squadron Officer.	*The Line will retire in Echellon of Squadrons from the Left.*	Obſervations.
*	*	No. 4. Threes about! March!	
	*	Halt! Drefs! March!	
		No. 3. ⎫	
		No. 2. ⎬ Repeated in fucceffion. (*a*)	(*a*) At a given diſtance by the commanding officer.
		No. 1. ⎭	
*	*	Form line on the right center (or fecond) fquadron.	
	*	No. 2. ⎫ Halt! Front! Halt!	
		⎧ No. 3. ⎪ Drefs!	
*	⎨ No. 4. ⎬ March! (*b*)		(*b*) No. 1. retires, halts, fronts, and dreſſes, by No. 2; 3 and 4 advance, halt, and drefs, by the fame fquadron.
		⎩ No. 1. ⎭	

Comm. Officer.	Squadron Officer.	The Line will attack to the Front.	Observations.
*	*	Right center (or second) squadron the squadron of direction—— March! Trot! Canter! Charge! Halt! (a) Dress!	(a) Flank serjeants and squadron officers aligne themselves to correct the line by the directing squadron.

Comm. Officer	Right Wing		Left Wing		*The Line will retire and form two Columns.*	Obfervations.
	Squa. Officer.	H. Sq. Officer.	Squa. Officer.	H. Sq. Officer.		
*	*				Right wing form column of half fquadrons, at quarter diftance, behind the adjoining half fquadron—Half fquadron, left eighth wheel! March!	
	*				Halt! Drefs!	
*	*				Three's left wheel! March!	
	*				Halt! Drefs!	
*	*				March!	
		*			Halt! Wheel up! Halt! Drefs! (a)	
*	*		*		The column will retire—Three's about! March!	(a) A fmall degree of left fhoulders forward is required in the formation of the column.
	*		*		Halt! Drefs!	
*	*		*		March! Halt! Front!	
	*		*		Halt! Drefs!	
*	*				The column will clofe to the front—March!	
		*			Halt! Drefs!	
*			*		Left fquadron, form clofe column of half fquadrons behind the adjoining half fquadron—Half fquadrons right eighth wheel! March!	
				*	Halt! Drefs!	
*				*	Three's right wheel! March!	
				*	Halt! Drefs!	
*				*	March!	
				*	Halt! Wheel up! Halt! Drefs!	

| Comm. Officer. | Right Wing | | Left Wing | | The Column will attack in Front and Flank. | Obſervations. |
	Squa. Officer.	H. Sq. Officer.	Squa. Officer.	H. Sq. Officer.		
*					Three's outward wheel!	
	*				No. 1, 2, 3, and 4, Three's, right wheel! ⎫ Repeated together.	
				*	No. 7 and 8, Three's left wheel! ⎭	
*	*		*		March!	
	*		*		Halt! Drefs!	
*	*		*		March!	
				*	No. 7 and 8—Halt! Wheel up! Halt! Drefs! March! Halt! Drefs!	
*			*		March!	
		*			No. 4, 3, 2, and 1—Right ſhoulders forward! Forward! Halt! Wheel up! Halt! Drefs! March! (a)	(a) Repeated by each half ſquadron officer, as they come to the ground on which they are to form.
*		*	*		Trot! Canter! Charge! (b) Halt!	(b) The right muſt regulate their paces ſo that both wings may finiſh the charge together

K

Comm. Officer.	Squadron Officer.	R. H. Sq. Officer.	L. H. Sq. Officer.	*The Regiment will retire in two Lines of alternate Half Squadrons from the Right.*	Obfervations.
*	*			Right center (or fifth half fquadron) the half fquadron of direction!	
*		*		Threes about! March!	
		*		Halt! Drefs!	
*		*		March! (*a*)	(*a*) The right wing retires in a circling direction, by bringing left fhoulders forward.
*				Halt!	
		*		Halt! Front! Halt! Drefs!	
			*	Three's about! March! Halt! Drefs! March! Halt! Front! Halt! Drefs! (*b*)	(*b*) The retreat is continued in this manner till the commanding officer wifhes to form line.
		*		Three's about! March! Halt! Drefs! March!	
*		*	*	Form line! (*c*)	(*c*) On the half fquadrons moft retired.
		*		Halt! Front! Halt! Drefs!	
	*			Eyes front!	